Living North of Lucky

Living North of Lucky

Erik Gingles

Community Books
Lockeport, Nova Scotia

Cover photographs and design: Erik Gingles
Book layout: Brenda Conroy
Proofreader: Michèlle Raymond
Printed and bound in Canada
by Hignell Printing Ltd.

Published by Community Books
Lockeport, Nova Scotia, B0T 1L0
ph/fax (902) 656-2223, email ktudor@atcon.com
www.outdoorns.com/communitybooks

Canadian Cataloguing in Publication Data

Gingles, Erik

Living north of Lucky

ISBN 1-896496-13-X

1. Japan — Description and Travel — Humor. 2. Japan — Social life and customs — 1945- — Humor. 3. Gingles, Erik. 4. Gingles, Caroline. 5. Canadian wit and humor (English). I. Title

DS812.G55 1999 952.04'9'0207 c99-950064-3

For Caroline . . .

who gave me Katherine

and everything else worthwhile.

Contents

Introduction

Most people today lead hectic lives with minuscule amounts of time to spare. Finding a bit of free time to read a book has become somewhat of a luxury, so you don't want to blow it on just any old book. The question you may ask yourself then is, "Why read *this* book?" Good question.

Well, odds are that if you're reading this page, you've already bought the book so you might as well read it. If you haven't and are thumbing through it at the bookstore, you've probably by this time unintentionally creased the cover and the guilt alone of doing that should be enough to make you take it to the counter and buy it. Once you have, you might as well go ahead and read it. Finally, if you're reading this at an acquaintance's house, you'll never know what helpful gems of trivia might be inside that they will know, but you will not. In which case, you'd best put this copy down and go out and buy your own copy immediately.

Please note, this is not just a book on Japan per se, but about life. And life with its little ironies can be quite entertaining to someone else who has or hasn't suffered these same ironies.

I will tell you up front however, I am not an expert on the Far East nor do I pretend to be so. What you read is pretty much what I observed and in no way necessarily reflects the views held by my wife.

Thanks, and enjoy.

In the Beginning

Getting There

"I'm going to the bathroom."

"Well I might not be here when you get back."

"You better be."

"I might."

"You better be."

We had traveled for almost thirty non-stop hours. We were now in the main terminal of Tokyo's Narita International airport. We missed our family and friends and were questioning our wisdom in coming. We were tired and cranky. We were immersed in a foreign language and had no idea what anybody was saying. We didn't even have a place to stay for the first night.

Traveling long distance is stressful, to say the least, and we were at our max. We were no longer the bright, cheery people who boarded the plane in Montreal. We were pale, bleary-eyed and not feeling very co-operative. At this juncture, we didn't see each other as our 'favourite people.' After our last little hissed squabble as to where we should leave our bags, our future together possibly rested on one simple question: Would I be there when she got back from the bathroom?

I watched her walk down the tiled corridor and wondered how far I could get before she knew I was gone. Just then, however, she looked back, and with her tired face gave me a soft smile as if to say, "We'll be okay" or was it "I have your passport"? Regardless, my heart warmed immediately and there I was waiting when she came out.

Having joined forces again our first order of business was to get a roof over our heads.

The friendly English speaking people at the Japan National Tourist Association gave us a list of cheap accommodations. I began calling from the public phone asking slowly and methodically "Do … you … speak … English?" On the alphabetical list, I made it down to the 'Ks' before the front desk of Kimi Ryokan answered 'yes.' They faxed a map to the tourist office, and with that in hand, accompanied with loose directions on which trains to take, we set off.

Both of us were glued to the window of the train as we slipped past countless rice fields and the silhouette of Mt. Fuji. The fields gradually, then more rapidly, were replaced with urbanization. Two hours later, at ten p.m. on a Friday night, we arrived in one of the largest areas of Tokyo.

Surfacing from the wrong subway exit, we found ourselves in a small dark alley. It was easy to tell which way was the front of the station simply by following the noise, neon lights and the smell of beer.

The smell of beer permeated the humid 33° C night air. Reams of reeling, drunken salary men, after a long work week, were bustling back and forth in front of the station and its endless outdoor counter bars. We weren't in Kansas anymore. The neon was everywhere. I looked at Caroline for her reaction, but she was just sitting on the curb looking up at me with an expression of utter exhaustion.

"I'm not going any further. I'm sleeping here."

I seriously considered this until I noticed how many people were relieving themselves on the sidewalk.

"Uhm … The map says we're almost there. Let's go just a little further," I suggested wearily.

I carried my suit-bag on top of my backpack with the shoulder strap under my chin for balance, and in each hand, was a suitcase. In this way we slowly trudged our way through the bustling crowds to find the inn we'd call home for the next week.

After weaving our way through tiny streets and wrong ways, we found the brightly lit sign saying "Kimi Ryokan." It was a fairly small two-level building that had communal showers and sinks on each floor. The rooms themselves were small but clean and there was air conditioning paid for by inserting 100-yen coins every two hours. It wasn't big and it wasn't fancy, but we couldn't have been happier to call it home. We had arrived.

The very next day we were searching for gainful employment. The rules of our Working Holiday visa which we came to Japan on, stipulated that we had to have a return trip ticket and a bank certificate proving that we did indeed have $1500 each in our accounts. We got the statements for $2200 then immediately withdrew $1500 for our airline tickets. That left us with a whopping $700 each. At $75 a night, plus food, we'd have enough to skim by for ten days. The clock was ticking.

Fortunately Caroline is a woman. What I mean to say (besides the obvious for me) is that because of this fact, she was able to get a job two days later through the Working Holiday job centre in Tokyo. It was for a small private school in the city of Nagoya, Japan's third largest metropolis. They wanted a woman because the kids' classes were afraid of male teachers. The owner, a British woman named Mandy, paid for both of us to come down on the *Shinkansen* (bullet train) and give it a two week trial. The job came with a furnished apartment and, as I was allowed to be considered part of the furnishings, so we were set.

That was June of 1990. We were two years out of university and still undecided on what direction our lives should take. I had spent a year working as a salesman for a transportation company, which didn't work out so well. It's down on my resume as 'the dark year.' After that, I spent a year doing freelance work for the regional CBC Radio station. That was much more to my liking, but not conducive to my bank account. We were both at the same juncture in our lives and wanted something different. Regardless of how small technology had made the world, we knew there was lots to see and we wanted to sample some of it. Then we heard the call, 'Go East.'

Granted, this 'call' was a little confusing to us, considering we were already living 'out East.' That being the East Coast of Canada, but what the call meant was for us to go even further East. To go as far east as possible before you started coming back. That was Japan.

We had heard about teaching English there a few years previously and it was always in the back of our minds as something would be 'kinda neat' to do. Japan was the kind of place that you always knew was out there, but never really expected to go to. A far-away land of electronics and gadgets and little plastic doo-dads. Here was our chance to see and experience another part of the world. An exotic place so different from where we were. A place so unlike home that big fat naked men wearing thongs were idolized.

We told ourselves we'd give it a whirl for six months, a year at the most, and then we'd be home. "Ha," we thought, "What's a year?"

We arrived in Nagoya on a Sunday. On Monday, the largest of the daily English newspapers, *The Japan Times*, was full of English teaching jobs. That very Monday I called three schools listed for Nagoya, had three interviews, and received three job offers by that afternoon. I don't kid myself into thinking I was something special in the English-teaching world, but at that time, it was just that easy. I took a job with a large school called Time that sent teachers to companies like Honda and the Fuji Bank on a daily basis. With no special training, I became a teacher of the English language. My visa even reads 'Specialist in the Humanities.' Can you imagine? Pretty scary when you think that on my first university English essay my professor wrote: "You've got some interesting ideas, but this paper is full of grammatical errors. If this is the best you can do, you've got some serious problems."

And now, I was being paid to pass on my wisdom.

I'm Big!

I soon found that as a language instructor, one has a great responsibility. We have to be alert to the 'garbage in, garbage out' phenomenon. In this regard, whatever you may tell a student will more than likely be repeated in the future. Whether you are joking or not, your students are apt to believe you hook, line and sinker. And why not? After all, you are the honourable *sensei*. I, however, would never intentionally lead a student astray, no matter how tempting it might be. Sure it could make for a good laugh, but I would more than likely be laughing all the way out the door, never to return, once they were privy to the real meaning to some of these idiomatic gems.

But what is good for the gander is also good for the goose. Just because I wouldn't do that to someone, doesn't mean someone wouldn't do it to me.

From the following little episode, I learned early never to repeat anything someone tells you to if you have no idea what you're saying.

As I mentioned, Caroline and I lived in the third largest city in Japan, called Nagoya. It's an industrial port city of a little over two million people and in the summer time, temperatures could reach a very humid 40° Celsius. For the first three months of our life in Japan, we lived in the apartment provided with Caroline's job. It was located over a fancy little coffee shop with some mighty tasty cakes. After being in there every day, the owner (or 'Master,' as restaurant owners are referred to in English), and I became good friends. He was a very likeable, pudgy little guy in his early forties. He had slicked back hair, mod glasses and was prone to wearing Hawaiian shirts while riding around on his huge Harley Davidson motorbike. You couldn't help but smile when you looked at him. Yet our current friendship got off to a rather peculiar start.

Caroline's first boss, Mandy, had been living in Japan for quite some time. The little English-language school that she owned was just around the corner from the coffee shop and our apartment. The Master and she had been friends for awhile. Upon our arrival in Nagoya, Mandy showed us to our apartment above the cafe. After pointing out where everything was, and how to use the gas burners to heat up the tub, etc., we headed down to be introduced to her friend, the Master.

The shop was rather upscale, with gentle jazz music in the background, lots of little mood lights and dark wooden chairs and tables. Caroline and I just sat there and tried to look intelligent as it was explained to the proprietor who we were and what we'd be doing for work. We dutifully smiled when our names were mentioned and that was about it.

When we finished our drinks I wanted to thank the Master for the coffees and cakes, which were on the house. Mandy was only too eager to oblige.

"If you're really grateful for something, bow low like this." She demonstrated by placing her hands palm-down on the counter, bringing them together, making the shape of an 'A' with her index fingers and thumbs. Next she touched her forehead to fingertips and continued with her instructions.

"Now say, *'Boku wa ooki desu.'*"

I got the Master's attention, then following Mandy's instructions to a 'T,' bowed, and muttered most sincerely the phrase of appreciation.

I looked up expecting to see a smile of gratitude, but only saw total confusion.

"Say it again!" Mandy prompted.

"Boku wa ooki desu."

Same thing.

I had no idea what I was saying wrong, or maybe the formation of my hands on the counter was a rude gesture in this country. Finally the Master stopped polishing a glass and responded.

"Boku wa chiisai, demo katai desu."

An answer. But what did he say?

"He said that he was small, but very hard."

"He's what?"

"He's small, but very hard."

Caroline was looking away and trying to distance herself from me. Mandy was making a marginal effort not to laugh directly in my face, and the Master continued to polish the glasses unperturbed.

"What?"

"Well … you told him that you were very … big."

"Big?"

"Yes, that's right. Big. In a manly sort of way."

"I see. Can we go now?"

We did. And from that point on, I vowed never to repeat anything anyone says in a language I do not understand.

I suppose the only saving grace is that Mandy didn't have to use the word 'big.'

Mistaken Identity
or
McEnroe Does Japan

Even after our very personal beginning, the Master and I did become good friends. With my schedule I was quite often free in the afternoons. Many times I would sit at the counter of the coffee shop, and watch the world go by outside the open glass doors that opened to a small tiled terrace out front.

In the evening, when the shop was quite busy, one of the Master's favourite jokes was to tell people that I was John McEnroe. Now, this is not something that I necessarily take as a compliment. If someone was watching me play tennis and said, "My God, he's looks like John McEnroe out there!" then I would be pleased. But just sitting inside a cafe and having someone say it, didn't have the same impact. I have to admit, at that time I did resemble John McEnroe somewhat. The nose and eyes helped, but my hair is what did it the most. I didn't have the mop-top he had when he was playing Borg at Wimbledon, but it was curly and receding, just a little.

So, if the Master smiled to one of his customers as he brought over his cake and said, while motioning to me, "That's John McEnroe over there," I'd play along. It was a good gag but one never carried on for more than five seconds. What the heck would John McEnroe be doing by himself in a small cafe in the middle of some industrial Japanese city anyway?

Around Christmas time though, I was waiting for Caroline to finish work around the corner and then join me. It was about nine-thirty at night and I was sitting at one end of the dark wood counter, talking away with the Master, when a nicely dressed young Japanese woman came in and sat at the other end. When he went over to take her order I heard him mention John McEnroe's name. On cue, I looked up and motioned for him not to embarrass me. He quickly apologized and hurried over to refill my water glass, leaving the young woman staring over in my direction.

I could feel her gaze quite heavily on the side of my face. I turned and nodded politely. She blushed, smiled and nodded back. I was waiting for the Master to tell her it was only a joke, as she seemed to think I was the real McCoy. After all, he had started the joke. He left me for her and they started chatting away. I could hear her ask him if I was really McEnroe. I expected him to come clean, but he didn't. The joke had moved to another level. It had become reality.

I was mortified because she obviously bought the schtick and would feel mighty embarrassed if she knew the truth. Every time I looked towards the door for Caroline, I could see her staring at me, smiling away. I felt terrible, but smiled back and then glowered at the Master who was too busy laughing out of her line of sight, behind his cake display.

I should have known this would not end easily. Caroline finally arrived, and so I thought would our departure. But as we had been talking about this John McEnroe phenomenon that very afternoon, Caroline came into the coffee shop, and said with a smile, "Sorry to keep you waiting ... John."

Crap.

This greeting just brought another burst of smiles from the young woman, and a water-letting from the Master. We'd gone way past the point of no return.

I managed to explain everything to Caroline under my breath and instead of commiserating with me, she joined the Master's side by saying "John" whenever she could.

"Would you like more water John?" or

"What do you want to do tomorrow, John?"

Nice, eh? We couldn't leave because Caroline wanted to wait for a co-worker before we went for a late dinner. Then, out of the corner of my eye, I saw a movement.

Having finished her coffee and cake, the young woman made what appeared to be a move for her wallet. Instead, what came out of her handbag was a notebook. "Oh no! Don't!" I said to myself. "Please don't." But she did.

Timidly she came over to where we were sitting.

"I play tennis!"

"Oh … uhm. That's good."

"Please … your sign?"

"Oh … oh, sure."

I dared not look at the Master or Caroline. Then, with confidence and bravado, I thought, "Sure. Why not?" With a dramatic sweeping motion I signed on a forty-five-degree angle, covering the page of her small note book, a flourishing, 'John McEnroe.'

I figured that if I had never seen his autograph, then she probably hadn't either.

"Thank you so much," she said in halting English. "I hope you have best Christmas ever!"

Quickly she left the cafe, backing up the whole way while continuing to bow until she was out of the door.

It was not a very nice thing to have done to someone who seemed like a very nice person. It was a joke gone awry that could have greatly hurt an innocent person's feelings. I regret having taken that chance. The only positive thing is that somewhere out there is a tennis fan who was made happy thinking that she met the real McEnroe. I hope she (and John) never know the difference.

Labels

It seems to me that one of the most important aspects in the younger Japanese consumer psyche is brand names. If it doesn't have a brand name, it has no value. Although the same can be said about the North American consumer, the average young working person in Japan usually has more disposable income than their counterparts on the other side of the ocean. This is due to younger people living at home rent-free until they're married, or living in subsidized company housing. The extent of this fascination with brand names became apparent to me, as most things did, in the Master's coffee shop.

On one of the many evenings that I sat there waiting for Caroline to finish her classes, a man in his mid-thirties sitting next to me struck up a conversation in English. While talking, he held his hand in front of his face. It was difficult to understand what he was saying, as his words were being muffled by his wrist. Not only that, but he kept angling the face of his watch so it remained directly in my line of vision whenever I talked to him. Finally, my eyes narrowed for a closer look at the watch that was being flaunted unabashedly. Once I made out the name (Patek Phillipe), he instinctively moved his wrist from his face, and now angled it towards the Master as we continued our conversation.

Being label-conscious goes part and parcel with the assumption that high price means high quality. It is not uncommon for young men to flip their ties over their shoulders so as to expose the 'Armani' or other designer label regardless of how hideous the tie may look. It's a status thing.

More recently, portable telephones the size of a box of wooden matches have become all the rage, and you must be seen talking into one even if you've got no one to call.

Television reported a fad about a year ago in which young people in Tokyo were paying up to $1,600 U.S. for a pair of 1970s Nike running shoes. Japanese entrepreneurs were scouring the California countryside buying up old, smelly Nikes and New Balance shoes, only to sell them for $800 to $1,000 U.S. in Japan. Status is based on what costs the most.

Status through possessions is not something that is limited to the average worker. Having designer bags to go with school uniforms is something that sets the average student apart from classmates. To support their habit of buying high-priced status symbols, some young girls have paid dates with older business men in exchange for cash (up to $800 to $1000) or presents. More of these girls are now in the junior high school range.

A not so drastic example, and perhaps more typical, was when a student of mine purchased a portable dual cassette CD player. There were three stores in town that sold that particular model, at quite substantially different prices. At a prestigious electronics store, the stereo was 15% more expensive than at a rather large mid-range department store. That store in turn was 15-20% more expensive than an all-round discount store. My student bought his stereo in the mid-range shop. His reasoning followed the price-scale-to-quality ratio.

He agreed that the prestigious store was gouging a bit, and it was more than he was willing to pay. The cheapest store was simply too cheap and hence, the quality was compromised in some way. He honestly thought that, even though the CD player was the same product in a sealed box, it had to be defective if it was sold at that price. This only left one viable option: the midrange store, where, by the way, it cost seventy dollars more than at the discount shop.

The Generous Homeless

Regardless of this country's advanced socio-economic situation, there are homeless people in Japan. With 125 million people, someone's got to be left unceremoniously out in the cold.

Since the bursting of the bubble economy towards the end of the eighties, and subsequent economic slow-down, there is a small, but growing number of people who've lost their homes. Some of these people had overextended themselves financially and could not pay off their loans when the banks called them in. As a result, a number of them are now living out of cardboard boxes at the big stations in downtown Tokyo. The difference with these station-dwellers, according to one TV report, is that they still have their jobs and continue to go to work wearing a suit and tie. It's just that now they live in a box. Naturally, that would make it a little difficult to bring the boss home for dinner.

"That was a lovely pot roast, Mrs. Yamamoto. Now, if you'd be so kind as to point me in the direction of the washroom ...."

"Of course. Go through the turnstile and it's just next to the southeast exit on your right."

Actually, they aren't married men, according to the report. More often than not, they are young single men not wanting to fall back on their families. They are trying to save enough money to pay all the initial fees required to rent an apartment, which can run up to several thousand dollars.

All the homeless are not in this situation of course. There are still your traditional 'abodingly challenged' people milling about with scraggly beards, tattered clothes, and muttering to themselves. And it was one of these guys that I had the distinct pleasure of having a drink with.

I have said that while in Nagoya, I was working at an English teaching company. They would sell a three-month course of English lessons to other companies in the area, and then we would go to their offices once or twice a week to teach their staff. One day you'd find yourself at a bank, the next at a trading company. Every Wednesday, four of us teachers would travel together on the train for an hour to the Honda factory. It made for a long day and we were always quite relieved to be on the train heading home come supper time.

Usually, when we reached Nagoya station, my friend Rudy and I would buy a few beers and some snacks from one of the station's kiosks, with whatever money we could scrounge from the bottom of our bags (this was only a few weeks after our arrival in Japan and things were still a little lean). We'd then sit outside the station on a bench watching all the people come and go in the humid summer evening. There were always a few homeless guys shuffling about, mumbling and chattering to each other and keeping pretty much to themselves. I never noticed any of them ask anyone for money, so it was a bit surprising when one guy came over this particular Wednesday and squatted cross-legged in front of us.

He was about forty-five to fifty years old. Underneath his soiled and baggy navy-blue windbreaker seemed to be a rather frail body that wouldn't take much more. He had a baseball-like cap on his head, placed jauntily to the side and tilted back. The gray stubble on his saggy face matched the colour of his wispy tousled hair. His pants were nondescript workman's pants in much the same condition as his windbreaker, and his sockless feet were doing a poor job of filling the canvas sneakers he was wearing. His eyes were muddy and surrounded by wrinkles. We couldn't tell if he had any teeth or not, but assumed he must have, if the traces of food all over his clothes and around his mouth were any indication. Looking at him would make a neatness-freak insane. I'm sure they'd have an irresistible urge to pull out that Kleenex from their sleeves, and wipe the goo from the corners of his mouth.

Shortly after he plunked himself down in front of us, he looked up and motioned for a cigarette. We slapped our pockets a few times and shrugged an apology to show that we didn't have any. He nodded in recognition and dropped his head to his chest and stared with his eyes half closed at a spot on the ground somewhere between his legs. A few moments passed and then he looked up and extended his hand towards my beer can.

"Not a chance my friend," I thought, while looking the goo around his mouth. Rudy felt the same and wouldn't hand over his beer either.

Immediately we felt guilty. After a few minutes of guilt-ridden silence, we reached into our bags and scoured the bottoms and pockets for any loose change. We came up with 285 yen ($2.50), a bit short of the 300 yen needed to buy a can of beer at the kiosk. Apologizing to him in a language we assumed he didn't understand, we motioned that that was all we had and to please take it, hoping somehow he could make up the difference.

Slowly, (with a little assistance from us), he got up, weaved his way into the station's main building and was soon out of sight. Rudy spoke first.

"Finally. I couldn't stand him looking up at me with those eyes, but there was no way he was getting a drink from my can. Not with that stuff all around his mouth."

So for 285 yen we had tried to buy off our conscience and demonstrate to the common man what benevolent guests we could be in their country.

Our friend was back in under ten minutes, sporting a plastic bag from the kiosk. Without a word he plopped back down in front of us and started to rummage through his stuff.

Our albatross had returned to roost.

To our surprise and shame, he produced not one, but three cans of beer. One for each of us. He dispensed them without hesitation, popped his open, lit up a smoke, and then proceeded to pass out right in front of us on top of his burning cigarette.

We sat there staring at our new benefactor, who, by this time, had curled into a ball and was muttering away in his sleep. Obviously our friend was not concerned in the least that the smoldering ember from his cigarette was probably making one doozie of a hole in his windbreaker.

Well-dressed passers-by would stop and apologize to us for this inexcusable act of civil disgrace and then try to wake up the sleeping figure by prodding him with the toes of their shoes. We intervened as best we could and assured the concerned citizens that he was no bother.

"Yeah," Rudy said with his thickest North Carolina accent, "He's our man." Soon people walked by with only a minor glance at the scene as two foreigners sat and watched over a sleeping 'bum.'

Twenty minutes later, he woke up and sat crossed-legged in front of us again. We smiled. He smiled back. With that, he picked up the rest of his things, raised his still full can of beer in a silent toast, got to his feet, seeming quite refreshed after his snooze, and ambled off somewhere into the night.

People to see, places to go.

In the three weeks left of our course at the Honda factory, we never saw our friend again. We both carried enough change to return the favour, but never got the chance. I suppose that's what kindness is all about: doing something for someone, and not expecting anything in return. As Rudy said, "He's our man."

And he was.

Getting to Nagano

Within a short time, both of us had adjusted to our new surroundings and settled into a regular work routine. We liked our apartment, we liked our jobs, we liked Nagoya. Then I got a call.

Downtown there is an International Centre where I had posted my name and number on the bulletin board to teach private English classes for extra money. At that time, a company called Fuji Electric (no relation to the film company) was searching for a full-time English teacher to instruct their staff. The position was at their Matsumoto factory in Nagano-ken. As their previous teacher, Don, had decided to teach at their Tokyo factory, they needed someone to fill the job and had asked a small private school to help them find a replacement. That school in turn asked a friend in Nagoya to help. That person (Tom) in turn went to the International Centre and got numbers from the bulletin board. Then he called me.

He explained that he was looking for a teacher on behalf of a large company called Fuji Electric and was I interested in the job.

"No. I'm not. Thanks anyway," was my response. I didn't know this guy, I didn't know Fuji Electric and I had no idea where Nagano was. Things were fine in Nagoya, and we had no intentions of moving after having finally gotten settled where we were.

As fate should have it, within a few weeks, two things changed our minds: a potential free lunch at the Nagoya Hilton and the questionability of Mandy's mental state.

We were living in Mandy's old apartment. When we first arrived, Mandy had moved in with her boyfriend, who owned a very high-end stereo shop. This was not some 'Wacky Watanabe's' discount store, but one that only needed to sell one or two stereos a month in order to remain wealthily afloat. Living in Mandy's place was a convenient arrangement, and one that had saved us a lot of money.

In Japan, in order to rent an apartment, you have to pay a damage deposit and what amounts to a cash gift to the landlord. This is called 'key' money. Sometimes it can end up being six months rent in advance, with very little of it returned to you when you move out. As the tenant's name did not change for the apartment, we simply assumed the rent payments for Mandy when she moved out. This was not a problem, because technically the apartment was under Mandy's school's name.

Then Mandy threw a brick through her boyfriend's shop window.

Love can be a very fickle thing and can lead a spurned loved one to do irrational things. Like a brick through a shop window. Obviously things had gone sour in Mandy's relationship and to prove it she hurled the brick. Obviously she would be moving out and we were crossing our fingers that she didn't plan to take over the apartment. As it turned out, she decided to move back to England and sold the school. To her stereo shop boyfriend no less.

At this time, Tom, still calling to see if I had changed my mind, (he must have been desperate to find someone) said that people from Fuji Electric were coming to do interviews at the Nagoya Hilton. Could I meet them at lunch time?

Not exactly being flush with cash, I thought that a free lunch at the Hilton would be a nice bonus regardless of whether I was interested in the job. I agreed without much of a second thought and arranged to meet them in the lobby of the hotel two weeks later.

The sequence of events during the next few weeks were a little confusing. The new owner of the school (Mandy's old stereo shop boyfriend) was using the profits from the school to help finance a second store he had opened in Tokyo. Not exactly the best timing, as it was just when the effects of the burst bubble economy were being felt and the demand for stereos the price of most family cars was diminishing. More and more money was taken out of the school and being poured down the drain in Tokyo. Repairs to the classroom were being ignored and salary payments were starting to get a little late.

The writing appeared to be on the wall that the school was not long for this world. I was mulling over our situation on the day I was to have the interview. If Caroline lost her job, we'd lose the apartment and would have to fork out a large sum to get another one. Not only the money, but finding a landlord who would rent to a foreigner was a tricky task in itself. The interview was becoming a little more than a free lunch in importance. In my head, I imagined what it would take for me to accept their proposal (if offered) and move to Matsumoto. With that in mind, I turned the corner to the hotel and opened the door.

Tom met me just inside the door and he ushered me to the side, whispering that we had to wait while they interviewed other candidates. I was a little crushed. I thought Tom only had eyes for me. Seeing that there were other people vying for the same position, I started to get a little more interested in the job and a little more worried about the situation in Nagoya.

We passed the time chatting while I kept an eye on the interview in progress. Much to my chagrin, the interviews were not 'over' lunch as I had thought, but 'at' lunchtime. Within a few minutes, it was my turn.

During the course of the interview, the people from Fuji Electric explained all about the job, where the factory was, and what they were willing to pay, etc. It was spooky. Everything was exactly, down to the last number, what I had imagined in my head before the meeting. Now I really wanted this job and did everything I could to restrain myself from dropping on the floor and begging them to give it to me. In due course I was thanked without any indication of how it went, and was told they'd 'let me know.' I hate that. Why can't anybody tell you now? I thanked Tom and reluctantly left.

Back outside in the humid 38° C sunshine I slowly walked to the nearest subway station, thinking maybe I should have begged, and wished minor ills on the other candidates.

Caroline was still at work when a call came from Tom later that very afternoon. Simply, I was in! Ha! Maybe they sensed I was willing to beg and that was enough to sway them. Either way, we were (or I was) moving to Matsumoto. My company at the time understood it was an opportunity not be passed up and wished me well. When Caroline's contract was over in a few months, she'd join me. It was all set. I packed up my knapsack again and took the three-hour train ride to central Japan, which would be home for the longest time since I moved out of the house for university when I was eighteen.

Matsumoto

Matsumoto is nicknamed 'The Belly Button of Japan' because it is almost exactly in the centre of Honshu, the largest of the four main islands that make up the country — not because there's an abnormal amount of lint here. It is also a castle town, and houses in the city centre one of the few original castles left in Japan. When we first arrived, there was a small digital countdown clock above the station in amongst all the billboards and neon. It was ticking off the days until the castle's summer-long 400th anniversary celebration. At the time, we didn't expect to see the clock reach the single digits. It was set at 762 and that was just too far into the future for us to plan. For the moment, we were content with the present which meant getting settled into our new neighbourhood, called Kotobukikita. Directly translated into English it means, North Lucky. What better place to be?

The city is part of the Shinshu basin which is a valley with a five-mile wide floor. It's a flat area that is renowned for its rice, grapes for wine, and apples. The area is nestled right up against the Japanese Alps, home to the '98 Winter Olympics. I'm sure many of you are unaware that Japan has its own Alps. It's rumoured that Sony bought them from the Swiss in the early eighties when the Japanese economy was at its zenith.

At their highest, the mountains on one side of the valley, known simply as 'The Alps,' reach up to a craggy snow-capped peak of over 3100 metres. Not quite the major leagues, as far as the European mountains (4500 plus metres) are concerned, but they're definitely in the game. The ranges nearby, while smaller than their European counterparts, are beautiful and spectacular to look at. On the other side of the valley are what's referred to as 'the mountains.' These are smaller than the Alps across the way, and don't reach above the tree line. Their highest peak is called Ustsukushigahara, or 'Beautiful Plateau' which it is indeed. From all areas of the city, the nub of Utsukushi can be seen looming close by.

The Nub, as I call it, is the highest point, or plateau on top, of Utsukushigahara. The summit is some 2000 metres above sea level and is home to a herd of roaming cows, something rarely seen given the price of land. From the front of the mountain, the Nub appears to be a large thumb-like outcropping of rock. However, having reached the top, you can see a huge sprawling pasture that spreads out for a kilometre towards the backside of the mountain, and down into a completely different valley.

Every spring there's a huge cattle drive to bring these bovines up the mountain to graze. And cattle drive it is. Japanese cowboys load up their wards onto trucks and then literally drive them to the top. Naturally, doing it this way does not allow for a 'Yee Ha!' scene. Not as spectacular as one may have imagined, but far more practical. In the fall, the reverse happens; thereby bringing the once wandering cows to their little cramped stalls in the outskirts of town where they'll stay for the winter.

Aside from being the highest mountain in the vicinity, Utsukushigahara is reputed to be an excellent vantage point from which to view the magnificent Mount Fuji on a clear day.

Or so they would have you believe.

The trick is to get up there on a clear day. I personally

believe there have only been seven recorded clear days since the dawn of time. And they were sometime just after or before Mount Fuji rose from the sea bed.

Anxious tourists need not fret about not being able to see Mount Fuji from the top of the Nub. In fact, I believe that almost every mountain and even every remotely tall building in the centre of Honshu, has the dubious honour of providing a view of Mount Fuji, on a clear day. Using the weather as an excuse is probably what many mountaintop gift-shop owners use to keep tourists coming back to their places of business in hopes of seeing it on a better day.

"Okay. Now look over there. See over there between those two mountains? If it was just a liiittle bit clearer, you could see Mt. Fuji. Come again tomorrow. It's bound to be better. And that will be fifty dollars for the film."

And so after a few failed attempts at seeing the magnificent Mount Fuji from the top of Utskushi, or any tall building for that matter, we decided it was time to leave our little valley for a weekend and investigate its existence.

Climbing Mister Fuji

*"A wise man climbs Mt. Fuji once in this lifetime.
A doofus will climb it twice."*

This ancient saying may seem Zen to those not having ventured up Fuji's slopes, but after having done it once, the meaning becomes a little clearer.

One of the few places where you'll most likely be able to see the 388-metre cone of a mountain is at its base. Unfortunately, even from the bottom there is no guarantee. On a fair number of excursions, to and from Tokyo's Narita airport, some five hours away from Matsumoto by car, we drove right past Mt. Fuji and on only a few occasions could we see it. Normally it was covered in a shroud of cloud. It's amazing. You can quite literally drive around the entire circumference of this natural spherical wonder that is visible from space with the naked eye, and never see the thing once. I think that is one reason why Mt. Fuji is considered in Japan to be a holy mountain. As it is rarely seen, you have to believe it's there, and not some secret government testing facility or a parking lot for some strip-mall.

Well, one day Caroline and I took the plunge with another couple to verify then and there for ourselves that Fuji-San, (loosely translated as Mr. Fuji) did indeed exist.

Picture if you will, hiking up a zig-zagging path devoid of any trees or vegetation, littered with disposable hand-held oxygen cans used for that quick shot of pure O_2 when the altitude gets a little much, and other assorted refuse. Imagine continuing this trek with an endlessly long, silent line of people with bowed heads, mostly throughout the dark, cold rainy night for six to eight hours, and then stopping for a short rest in a small dank mountain inn before making the final push to the summit, in hopes the clouds will part, allowing you to view the sunrise from the highest peak in Japan. Sound good? Go ahead, fill your boots.

As mentioned, Fuji-San is a volcano. And like most good volcanoes, is covered with lava rock. These rocks are excellent when found inside your gas barbecue, but not so excellent when you're trying to hike up almost 4000 plus metres on them.

It makes for a very bleak landscape. The only thing I could imagine growing on such forbidding soil would be the hardy lima bean. (Yes, the lima bean. The very same bean that when placed in the middle of a wet paper towel would sprout the next day. I used to wonder in elementary school, what cosmic freak of nature caused this life process to take place right on my very window sill, in the middle of some wet paper towel. As far as I was concerned, the more lima beans I could cram into the paper towel, the better. The more in there meant the less I had to eat. And not being an afficionado of lima beans, that was a good thing. Anyway, that magnificent marvel of growth, the lima bean, would perhaps be the only thing that would have the fortitude to grow on the side of a mountain covered with porous lava rock. A mountain of lima beans reaching to the sky. My worst childhood nightmare.)

So there we were, leaving the parking lot at the base of Mr. Fuji to begin our trek. The hike is not technically difficult, and therefore attracts all walks of life. The old, young, rich and poor. The fashionable, the shabbily dressed, the athletic and the overweight. But there was one common bond between all the hikers on that day. One thing made us all equal and that was the naiveté to think that doing this would be some kind of enjoyable and enlightening experience. True, a wise man will only climb Mt. Fuji once, but an even wiser man would never climb it at all.

The trek begins from the fifth station. A 'station' is the designated place from which your wallet is relieved of some of its bulkiness. The fifth station is just about where the tree line ends. It's the most common starting point. The base camp if you will. I've never heard of anyone starting below the fifth station. In fact, I don't know if there are any stations below the fifth. Regardless, people generally arrive at the station's massive parking lot by car or bus.

The main building here is quite impressive and distinctly 'Sound of Music-ish' in nature. Lots of white stucco and dark timber beams. Festive music is piped in and vendors of all sorts have countless souvenirs for sale. Bright colours are everywhere. Every individual gift shop has tons of post cards of Mt. Fuji at sunset, sunrise, noon time, and even the all black cards that say 'Mt. Fuji at Night.' Oddly, there are no cards of a cloud-enshrouded Fuji.

This whole area is exciting, pumping would-be climbers up for the hike. It's the doorway to the top of Japan. But like many attractions, the glamour and glitter of the outside entrance isn't necessarily indicative of what's on the other side. Going past the carnival-like atmosphere of the main building, you are met with the stark, colourless contrast of the lava rock trail out back. A climber may think they'll just go as far as the next station and turn back if things don't look any better. However, the sixth station is conveniently located quite far away from the starting point so by the time it's reached, you feel it's too late to go back. As it happens, after the sixth station, the rest of the pit stops are strung apart by only a couple of hundred metres, coaxing you further and further up the hill.

One item that we did buy in the parking lot was an official Mt. Fuji hiking staff for twenty dollars. At each of the rest stops on the way up, you can pay a buck to have a stamp branded onto your stick with that station's number and elevation. Collecting these brandings became an obsession with us. It was like being a kid and collecting baseball cards, except, unlike baseball cards, these staves were hard to keep in your pockets, were difficult to pin to the front wheel of your bike, and worse, you got no gum. In spite of that, we religiously waited in line at every stop to get our stamp. Only at the top could we stand there and appreciate our completed poles with pride. It never once crossed our minds at the time that that was perhaps the most irrational forty dollars we ever spent. The sixty dollars each we spent on our hillside accommodations was no sound Wall Street investment either.

It was late afternoon when our little entourage started out. After a few hours of trudging up the mountain, both the wind and the rain picked up just as what little light there was from the sun went down. We courageously kept on, and as comrades do in times of difficulty, did our best to lift each others spirits by giving words of encouragement such as "That octopus burger at the fifth station doesn't look so bad now," or "Boy, does this suck."

Finally we wearily made it to the fifteenth station, where we had reservations for the night. We had planned to stay here for only a few hours' sleep and then push on through the cold drizzle to reach the summit for sunrise. To our tired and now cold bodies, the soft glow of light coming through the window of the roughly hewn wooden shack off to the side of the trail was an inviting sight. Pulling against the wind whipping up the side of Fuji, we opened the door and piled in. Sanctuary at last.

The accommodations were, well, in a word ... smelly. It was a small wooden structure with a miniature pot-bellied stove in the middle for warmth. However, only if you sat right on top of the thing with your pants down around your ankles might you feel some inkling of heat coming from the few sticks of kindling inside. It was more for the ambience than a thing of creature comfort. There was also a sturdy wooden table at one end for eating, and on the other side of the stove, bunk beds against the walls.

When I say bunk beds, I really mean fifteen-metre-long plywood shelves jutting out from the wall, in two levels, separated by a one-metre space. You did not lie parallel to the wall as one might expect, but rather, at right angles and head first. This way, the people running the inn could get fifteen people crammed in per shelf. Unfortunately the plywood was not bare, but was covered with what appeared to be three-hundred-year-old futons that were cold and damp and smelled of moldy popcorn.

Sleep would not come quickly.

Not having much choice, I burrowed in head first and tried to block out the smell by breathing through the top of my turtleneck sweater. My compatriots seemed not to mind the fetid surroundings, if the sound of their raucous snoring was any indication.

Like most Japanese people, the hikers that I was squashed up against in this dark, musty tunnel of a bed, could fall asleep at the drop of a hat. It must be an inherited gene or something that's developed over decades of commuting to work by train. On early morning commutes, just as soon as those doors close, at least half of the heads drop like stones to their chests and are snoring in seconds. I am not one of those people, and resigned myself to merely resting and breathing through my turtleneck. I was strangely comforted by the howl of the wind and the sound of the rain being whipped against the outside window pane, as all except one slept soundly in the warmth of close, smelly quarters.

Sleep eventually came for me, but only long enough to allow me to be awakened to continue the dark trek in the rain with the faint hope of seeing the sunrise from the top.

Climbing Mister Fuji (Part Two): The Top

After eight and a half hours from the time we left the hut we unceremoniously made it to the top. At the end of the trail, someone was handing out white headbands with the red rising sun in the centre to all the nationals. We were not given one. Just before daybreak about 600 to 800 people, all sporting their newly acquired headbands (except for us and a few other foreigners shifting nervously about), faced the rising sun, and sweeping their arms up like gymnasts dismounting from the balance beam, shouted in unison the traditional yell of solidarity for all to hear.

"Bonsai ... Bonsai ... Bonsai!"

I had the uncomfortable feeling that some kind of sacrifice was about to be made to the volcano and maybe those without a headband were it. I felt a sudden appreciation for the heavy weight of my walking stick in my hands. The moment soon passed. The volcano god seemed to be appeased by a little shouting and we continued to be duly ignored.

With the normalization of my heart rate following the greeting of the sun, we toured around the top of Mr. Fuji. It's pretty impressive. Over the centuries the centre of the cone has filled in naturally with rocks and stones that have fallen towards the centre. The mountain last erupted in 1723, and given its general size, it must have been a doozie. Now, almost three hundred years later, there's a bit of a sunken pond to one side at the bottom of the crater, but the rest of the surface is covered with messages made out of white stones. Things like "Yasushi likes Yasuko" or "Eat Sushi at Yamamoto's."

While the volcano is not active, it is not considered entirely dormant either. Regardless, I did not feel the need to spend much time wandering around the white clusters of stones on top of what's perhaps the world's largest cork. In spite of the arduous, rainy climb, it turned out to be a beautiful day of crisp blue skies, but at 4000 metres above sea level, it was quite brisk to say the least. I was dressed in multiple layers to keep warm, which after sacrificing fashion for comfort, seemed the right choice. My smugness soon dissipated when I realized that I had to go to the bathroom. Normally this would not have caused me any deal of distress. I had become learned in the art of using the squatting-style Japanese toilet; however, the suspenders of my rain pants were foolishly buried under eighteen layers of clothes. Given the time it took for me to dress, the action of disrobing, then suiting up again seemed to be too much of an effort. Instead, I chose what turned out to be the more difficult option of the ole 'Pull and Drop' and headed into the cramped, dark outhouse.

The rickety structure reminded me of a shack in a Charlie Chaplin movie that was perched precariously on the edge of the mountain cliff. The only difference was that this shack was completely dark when the outside door was closed. As I mentioned, I am skilled in the art of using the Japanese toilet. For those of you unfamiliar with said device, I will try to explain it you as delicately as I can.

It's basically a ceramic trough with a 'backstop' at the front, standing about eight to ten inches above the 'bowl.' (*See Figure 1*)

Even unhindered by several layers of clothes and pants around your ankles, this is tricky business at best for the uninitiated. The biggest worries beginners usually have are a) "Am I lined up over the hole?" and b) "Am I going to poop

Figure 1

in my pants?"

At the top of Mount Fuji, I was dealing with a whole new set of problems. I was occupying one of the three available stalls. The outside door was shut, making it pitch black except for a few slivers of brilliant sunlight cutting through a few cracks in the wooden walls. No matter. I had a flashlight. It was, however, a flashlight which could not be stood on end. It had to be held, but I had no hands available to hold it. Both of my hands were busy straining under the incredible amount of resistance put forth by my heavy-duty three-inch-wide industrial suspenders. I was desperately yanking and pulling against the suspenders, doing my best to hold my pants between my legs, away from the 'drop zone.' I started to perspire. Doing isometric exercises in a plastic rain suit over layer upon layer of clothes in an enclosed area produces a significant amount of heat energy.

With no available appendages, I had no choice but to clench the flashlight in my teeth. If you try this at home you'll notice two things. One, clenching a large hard plastic tube in your teeth is far more difficult than you first thought. Two, this action also produces a phenomenal amount of drool. I have discovered during these circumstances that the amount of drool is directionally proportional to the size of the flashlight handle. The bigger the handle, the bigger the drool. Try it out.

So, I've got the light clenched in my teeth and go into the crouch. It was a one-shot deal and great care had to be taken not to drop the flashlight. If you did drop the flashlight, you wouldn't want to put it in your mouth again. With both hands I reached between my legs and once again pulled up on my rain suit pants, my sweat pants, and my long underwear, trying to bring the whole ensemble up somewhere between my knees. The eighteen layers I was wearing on top were bunched up in my lap, not allowing me a clear view. I had to 'go' on faith.

My next move was to position myself without stepping into the remnants of other's misalignments. That done, I relaxed the grip on my pants to give my arms a rest before the final ... (push?). I was getting hot. There was too much drool running down the flashlight. My legs were beginning to go numb after having been in this most unnatural of positions for too long.

It was now or never.

Just as I was about to pull up on my pants with all of my might, the door to my stall flew open and a kazillion-watt flashlight lit me up like a deer caught on the highway at night.

Everything happened at once. As I swiveled in panic to meet my intruder, I released my straining pants. They shot back into their original position like a rocket-on-rails, giving me one of the worst self-inflicted wedgies known to man. The momentum of my pants tipped me off balance just enough for my spasming legs to shoot forward, throwing me back against the wall and onto my bare butt with a big *ooomph!* and slobber all over the front of my jacket. When it was all over, the flashlight was left spinning like a disco light on the floor.

I pity the poor man who had to witness that. I recall the sound of a stifled yelp and of the door banging closed as the intruder whisked his young son away, hoping the scene wouldn't permanently scar his impressionable young mind. I'm sure from time to time he'll have nightmares of the 'white half moons' dangling in the air before they were swallowed up by some drooling, yellow-clad alien.

I was left with my own scars. They were more of the physical kind really, courtesy of the rough wooden wall of the outhouse as I fell against it. As for the other damage, well, that could all be fixed in the next washing at home. I told no one at the time about my little incident and once I was ready, we decided to descend. The descent was quick and uneventful and I gladly left the holy mountain, and a part of me, behind.

Corporate Japan

Freshmen and the Business Etiquette

As with almost all aspects of life over here, things have to be done in a certain way, and only that way. This could not be more apparent than in a large Japanese company.

The new employees all start work in the spring and are called in the company 'Freshmen.' The Japanese word for Freshmen is … *Freshmen*. Once they finish their two-month training which takes them to various factories within the company, they join a section. This section becomes like their family and they are referred to, in their first six months or so, as the 'New Face.' For example, an employee introduced a new member of the company to me, something like this: "Hello Mr. Erik. He just come to our section. He is New Face."

"Why hello there Mr. Face. How are you?"

New Face looks puzzled and looks from me to Suzuki and back to me.

"It was a joke!"

"We must go."

"They never get me."

Anyway, most New Faces for any corporation are hired in their third year of university. They are actively recruited by large companies who send alumni to talk to potential New Faces. Once these students have signed on the dotted line, they are the sole property of the company. Winter and Summer uniforms included.

The head of the section is the *kacho*, or Manager. A Manager is revered as a kind of father figure, and all the subordinates form the family pecking order according to their seniority in the company. And, like all Freshmen in a tight family-like group, the New Face is decidedly the Peon, coerced into doing a variety of menial office duties for the first couple of months.

Something that all New Faces must go through are obedience lessons. I'm not inferring that the managers have to put newspapers all over the floor for the first few weeks while the overexcited freshmen squirm and piddle in their summer uniforms. No, I mean (and I'm not kidding here), they learn a kind of pecking order obedience and etiquette.

Picture one hundred and seventy five people in the company's gym practicing their bowing. Seems simple enough, but the guys who are good at it always make it look easy. Here are 175 people bent over at the waist and holding the position while a bow master (?) goes around lifting a chin here and straightening a back there. Perhaps to the unknowing, this may seem like a waste of time, but for new employees, the angle of the bow changes from a forehead-bumping-on-the-ground kind of bow, to a casual nod of the head and shoulders depending on who is receiving said bow. On top of that, the really higher-ups not only get big bows, but they get more than one.

I think with all a New Face has to learn, there is undue pressure put on new employees to remember all of the moves in regards to bowing. Therefore, I have drafted for all Freshman, a Handy-Dandy Bow Chart that they can keep in their wallets. Should they spy a Vice President coming down the hall and are not sure what to do, they can simply refer to the card and relax. (*See Fig. 2*)

My first experience with such a bowing spectacle was when the President of Fuji Electric came to inspect the factory where

Handy-Dandy Bow Chart (*Figure 2*)

Mgr. Class	# of Bows	Angle of Bow	Duration	Other
Sect. Mgr.	1	45°	2-3 secs.	None
Dept. Mgr.	1	60°	hold for count of 4	Muttering something respectful is an option
Div. Mgr.	2	1st bow - 90° 2nd bow - 60°	2 secs. count of 4	Mutter something like "Great tie!" or "Have you been working out?"
Vice-Pres.	3	all at 90°	all for a count of 4	Continuous respectful mutterings are best. This cannot be overemphasized. Do not look up or move until you're sure he's gone. Note: be careful not to mutter anything that he may consider infantile.
President	unlimited	as low as you can go	as long as it takes	Under no circumstances should you you stop bowing or muttering. If you have advanced knowledge that the President is coming, do the "President's Bowing Warm-Up Stretches" found in your freshman manual. Those of you capable of bending far enough to kiss your buttocks will have a natural advantage over most. Those less nimble can make up for it with more emphatic muttering or maybe even whimpering. Be careful not to become annoying. Remain doing all of the above until the President has left the building and the "All Clear" signal is given on the factory's siren.

I work. My classroom had been a clean-room originally (one of those rooms where you have to wear a space-suit and should you break wind, would be responsible for contaminating billions of yen worth of semi-conductors). These controlled environment rooms have windows along the sides so people walking down the corridor can look in. Forgetting these windows can be embarrassing if you have the urge to scratch.

Nonetheless, on that particular day the company president was to visit. Through the windows I could see men lined up all along the corridor waiting for the Big Cheese. Everything gleamed. Hats were in hands as the employees, like kids, waited for Santa Claus to come at the end of a parade. I turned away for a moment to finish what I was writing on the white board. When I looked back, there he was striding down the hall all by himself. Our stern president swiveled his clean-shaven head from side to side as he muttered inaudibly. To whom he was speaking I could not tell. There wasn't a soul to be seen. Just the chief and me. As soon as he rounded the corner, forty heads and torsos bobbed up from below the window sill, broke ranks and scattered in different directions, leaving the hall empty again.

Now these guys must have been really bowing. I mean, for the president to have passed through that narrow hallway and not have kicked anybody in the head? That's flexible.

There are stories as to why or how the bow got started in the first place. It was said that a long time ago (naturally), if you wanted to show respect or gracious servitude to your master, you'd bare your neck so he could chop off your head if he so wished. As the ruling samurai class was the only group allowed to carry swords, you were much better off showing respect and baring your neck to a rice farmer than a samurai. With just one too many cups of the ole rice wine, he just might take you up on it.

Besides the bowing and learning the proper way of saying "Good Morning" and "Good Afternoon," in unison, the New Faces also get introduced to English.

My company has overseas factories in the Philippines, Scotland and the U.S. Hence, English-language study is the foundation of their plan of global economic conquest. Well, that's what I tell them when it's time to negotiate my yearly contract. So, after the grueling bowing seminars, it was my turn to impress on the new recruits how important the English language would be to their careers with the company. And what better way to introduce them to the English-speaking global family than through floor hockey. What better way indeed to hone the language fundamentals than with passing drills and checking techniques.

A friend named Sean from home very graciously shipped over thirty hockey sticks with broken blades donated by the local Montreal Canadians farm team. He included thirty plastic blades to make them useful. I spent four hours one night sawing off old blades and attaching the new plastic ones. Admiring my handiwork, I knew I was ready to teach English.

You may be trying to make the connection in your head between hockey and teaching English. Well, there isn't any. Yet there was a purpose to this activity. Most Japanese who have never met a foreigner (particularly if they don't come from a major metropolitan city), do one or more typical things on first encountering someone from away. They either: a) don't utter a sound; b) thrust a finger at you and shout *gaijin* (foreigner); c) turn around in circles until they fall down; d) speak better English than you do.

The bunch waiting for me in the gym were definitely the a) through c) types. In order to prevent a mass anxiety attack, I plotted to distract them with sticks. Teaching English was not on the agenda. Acclimatizing them to an actual, living, English-speaking *gaijin* was the simple goal for the day.

After having lined them up along the side of the gym walls, my lovely assistant Aaron, a young American music student at the Suzuki School of Music, handed out the newly crafted sticks. Immediately they started swinging them like the golf clubs they love so much. Naturally, some of the blades which were not affixed so well soon came off and were whirring around the gym like boomerangs. A fine start.

Being Canadian, holding a hockey stick was second nature to me. It never occurred to me that someone wouldn't know how. Even with all the bowing practice, it was the bending of the waist part that was eluding them, as well as the hand positioning. How was I ever to teach them English, if I couldn't teach them this?

"Okay everybody! Hold the end of your stick with your left hand, then put your right hand under the stick one third to half the way down the shaft."

I demonstrated and waited for all to follow my actions.

"Good. Now keep your left hand on the side of your hip, and bring your right hand about 30 degrees in front of you. Good. Now ... imagine your ... manager is coming!"

Clack! All thirty sticks went down at the same time.

You've just got to put it into terms that they can understand.

I feel I must admit publicly that I was never very good at hockey. I realize this may come as a bit of a shock to some of you, but as my coaches over the years will attest, I stunk. The main reason, besides lacking any skill or co-ordination, was a basic lack of body mass. At that age, those who were destined to play good hockey grew to be eight or nine feet — or so it seemed every time I picked myself up off the ice. Those of us who were more prone to being better at, say, racquet sports, remained at the five-foot level. But ironically, right here in this gym on the other side of the world, in the sweltering heat of a hot May afternoon, with young impressionable minds, I was the embodiment of hockey.

I dropped the orange sponge puck on the floor and there was an instantaneous flurry of movement and excited whispering that stopped as the puck rolled to a halt four feet away. Reaching over, I retrieved the puck with the tip of the blade. I stick-handled the puck back and forth as one hundred and fifty eyes followed. I stopped. The heads stopped.

Silence.

A cloud passed over the sun. A dog barked. Somewhere in Algeria a baby was born.

Now was the time.

Standing at one end of the hardwood-floored gym with two rows of eager students standing on either side, I unleashed a blistering wrist-shot. It was the first time I ever used a sponge puck and I must say, I was quite surprised at the lift it got. It sailed three feet lower than the top of the velvet wine coloured curtain that hung over the stage at the end of the gym like in most junior high schools. With a *thwoop* it hit the heavy curtain, hovered for a moment, then fell. Applause broke out. The freshman closest dropped his stick with a clatter, ran to the puck where it lay, picked it up, and then ran back to me with the puck in hand. I felt like I had bagged a mallard duck. I was unsure whether to thank him or scratch him behind the ears.

I waited for a few seconds for the hubbub to die down. It dawned on me that I was really soaking up this new-found hockey adulation. There they were, all smiling at me, thinking I must have been great back home at the game. Who was I to spoil that? Let alone point out the fact that the net is rarely twelve metres above the ice. No sir. Not today. Today, I was MR. ERIK, EIGO NO SENSEI (English teacher), SPONGE PUCK HOCKEY GURU.

It was short lived.

The Japanese catch on quickly to almost anything new. And when they've got it, they've got it cold. Floor hockey was no exception. We went from simple passing drills, to stick handling drills, to a scrimmage, to me getting my butt kicked by some of the more talented students.

My getting them used to interacting with a foreigner through hockey was a success. And so was the game itself. It quickly turned into a regular event and it was during our weekly Wednesday night games that I saw my star status quickly fade. What could I expect? Hell, I was still shooting the puck twelve metres over the top of the net, and it didn't take a genius from Gaul to figure out that I wasn't scoring any points for my team with this shot. To get back some of the glory, I started to introduce rules that I didn't point out earlier for simplicity's sake.

When they caught on to those rules and started running

circles around me, I started to introduce fictional rules. Such as, "When you're shooting towards the net at the south end of the gym, you can't pass forward. It must be a lateral or drop pass only." When I was called on it later in the game, I pointed out that it was now after seven p.m. and forward passes were now acceptable. Look it up if you don't believe me. Heh, heh.

I soon realized that my excuses were not so readily believed and there was dissension in the ranks. Power corrupts. But my eager charges learned to play the great game of hockey (minus the fisticuffs). Perhaps in more practical terms, they learned (as I did myself those first few days in Nagoya), not to believe everything anyone tells them.

Your New Company Family and Romance

So now the New Faces have been accepted into their new family fold with the manager acting as father. And like most families, they will go on vacation together.

At least three times a year, any given section will go on a weekend trip to some spa or hot spring resort. Once there they will all don a heavy cotton bathrobe/pyjama thing called a *yukata*, provided by the spas. They gather in a large *tatami* mat room, eat sushi, drink copious amounts of beer and sake while singing karaoke until four a.m. The thing is, no spouses attend. I don't know if this is a rule or not, but, as a matter of course, wives (or husbands, should that be the case) do not go. It's a section thing. Can you imagine what would happen if the average Western office worker told his wife that he was going away for the weekend with his manager and office girls for an all night pyjama party/booze fest?

"Oh, by the way, I completely forgot all about it until Bob from purchasing reminded me, but we have a weekend seminar starting this Friday night until Sunday on the socio-political ramifications of our new ST-5X series vacuums. Look, I know it's Grandma Pushkin's 80th birthday celebration at the Rotary Club, and it just sickens me to say this, but I just can't make it to her party this weekend all because of this damn seminar! I was really looking forward to it. You know

I was. But you know how it is at the office, Hon. The Boss says go, and you go. "

An eerie and menacing tone prevails.

"I'm sorry. I didn't catch everything you said. What was that?"

"Uhm … I … I said …"

"Yes?"

She slices through one of those fat German knackwurst sausages with the greatest of ease, using a HUGE kitchen knife on the cutting board, then slowly sweeping it into the sink's garbarator to watch it get mulched in front of our eyes.

"I …uh … was wondering if I should wear my green tie or my b… blue tie to Grandma's birthday party."

For some reason, married men in Japan don't seem to have any trouble with these spousal exclusion weekends. I think that it should be noted that 90% of married couples, whether young or old, sleep in separate beds. This is only a personal estimate based on a survey of the only five bedrooms I've seen mind you, but I have yet to see any bedroom with a double bed. Don't get the idea now that I go off into other people's bedrooms, but as most bedrooms are off the living room, it's easy to do a little recon. with a sweeping glance. If there is a correlation between twin beds and the all night party pyjama booze fests that men go to, I would be interested to know about it. It should be duly noted as well, that working married women as well quite readily attend their own section's pyjama parties, minus the hubbies.

Now, besides being the man in charge of developing a family-like relationship with his staff, the manager is also the company Cupid. It only makes sense when you think of it. For the most part, the staff works 25 hours a day, eight days a week. Who has time to go to bars and seek a mate? So romance flourishes in the office environment and is helped along by the manager.

In North America many young married couples first met

in school at one stage or another. If you think of a large company factory as a 'campus,' the idea of rampant company inbreeding seems a bit more natural.

For example, the factory in Matsumoto where I work is about the size of a small college campus. There are two or three gates from which to enter. Each employee has an ID card which they must show to the guards at one of the gates. There are four lit tennis courts, a baseball diamond, a soccer field and a brand new gym complete with a hi-tech stereo system to pipe music everywhere. The spotless showers provide soap, shampoo and towels. There is a beautifully decorated lounge with free green tea. There's also a massage service for employees with stiff shoulders or backs. And a bright, sunny infirmary with a full-time doctor and staff. A cafeteria and a small building filled with banking machines grace another side of the factory. After you withdraw some money, you can go to the small store which sells anything from pastries to personal computers. They even have a car dealership come into the factory in the spring to show off some of the new models.

Just outside the compound walls and across the street are the dormitories which are generously subsidized by the company. There are at least four buildings for the males and three for the females. The Freshmen get a roommate for the first year in the company. They all eat dinner in the dining hall. They elect an executive committee, which always includes a social chairman whose responsibility is to arrange social functions with the female dormitories. If you get married, you can move into the 'married couples' dormitory up the street, or spend a little more for your subsidized housing and get a more exclusive company apartment elsewhere in the city.

It is a self-contained functioning society. Why go anywhere else? Working in the evenings then is like going to the library after supper in university. There are no professors hovering over you and you're free to get up and move about the floors talking to friends and checking out the action. By action I mean how the semi-conductor wafer process is coming along. Some people, as in the library at school, are there to work. The rest of us are into the wafer process. In such cases, a meeting of two lonely souls may happen while suiting up for the clean room, or maybe even over an offer to look at private wafers in one's dormitory.

"Oh come on!" you're probably saying. "Give us a break. Nobody falls for the 'come to my room and see my wafers' routine anymore." Well, don't be fooled, my friend. It could happen, and probably does more often than you think. Whatever the case, the dating scene over here is clouded in mystery and secrecy. You rarely ever know if someone is dating. You can constantly ask your students what they did on the weekends, etc. and you will always get the same two answers. "I went driving" or "I slept."

"You mean to tell me that you slept both days?

"Yes."

"You didn't go to the bathroom or anything? Just stayed in bed aaall day?"

"Yes."

"By yourself?"

"Yes."

Nobody says they had a date. Nobody. Even if asked directly, "Did you, or did you not have a date this weekend?" the inevitable response is "No." Like clockwork. Then one day a different answer appears.

"So, what did you do this weekend. Wait! Let me guess. You slept?"

"No. I got married."

I'm telling you it happens all the time. People usually don't tell anybody they're dating, let alone say they're planning to get married. I've been told that they don't say anything because if it doesn't work out, they'd be embarrassed and lose face with their co-workers. Hmm.

If it does work out after the first few months, it's not uncommon for the couple to be picking out patterns or getting registered at their favourite sushi bar.

Only a skilled eye can detect the subtle nuances of romance in the Japanese office. The knowing glance. The casual bump next to the photocopier. The way she pours his green tea first, or the way he knocks the books out of her arms. It's a little less subtle in North America when some yop yells out "Hey baby! Let's bump uglies!" Granted, this approach does alleviate a lot of time-consuming guess work.

A system that is not as vulgar as the yop's mating call, but just as succinct, is the good old-fashioned arranged marriage. This is not the kind done at birth. In today's society, neither the man, nor the woman, is forced into an arranged marriage. The pressure from the family to get on with it however, can be pretty intense.

In the current system of arranged marriages, the customers submit their resumes to a match-making company. In it they state their interests, ideas about work and raising a family, along with a current photo. Next, a meeting is arranged with the service's counsellor to help the male customer pick out a likely prospect. When the client selects a resume, (largely based on the accompanying photo), the selectee is then contacted by the agency, and has the inquirer's stats sent to her to see if she would like to accept the proposed meeting. If all parties are in agreement, then a date is set up, usually for coffee or dinner. Personally, if it were me, I'd cut out a picture of Brad Pitt and stick it on my resume. I may not get the second date, but at least I'd have a night on the town with the woman of my choice.

If nothing tremendous happens on the first date, but a second date is acceptable to both parties, it too is arranged by the company's counsellor. After that, you're more or less on your own. If the final outcome of these meetings is a marriage, the company takes a sizeable fee from both parties. Nice work, eh? The dating period is relatively short in these situations because both parties know that the other one is into getting married. Otherwise, they wouldn't have sent resumes in the first place. But that isn't always the case. Sometimes they are submitted purely to get mothers off backs. The incessant chant of "Get married" by some mothers can be relentless. It increases in intensity and frequency every year after the 25th birthday. There must be some holdouts however, as I read that Japan has the second highest average marrying age for women anywhere in the world at the ripe old age of 27.3. These figures may imply that many are choosing a career over marriage, but, from what I've seen, I don't think that's the reason.

While North America still has a long way to go for real equality between men and women in the work place, it is still better than the situation in Japan. It is rare to find a woman manager in a company of any size, even in bigger cities like Tokyo and Osaka. Younger women make photocopies and tea. It's a vicious circle.

The company knows that when a young female employee gets married, she's more than likely going to quit. So they don't consider that particular resource pool for advancement. Why spend the money training them if they are going to quit? However, the young female employee wants to quit because a lifetime of making photocopies with no prospects of advancement isn't all that appealing. Therefore, for many women who have little chance of climbing the corporate ladder, marriage and raising a family is a better alternative. In a way, it is a career move. If they marry a decent enough guy with a decent enough salary, they can quit the company and run the house. The beauty of this situation for all would-be brides is that once joined in matrimony, the wife controls all of the household income. I mean all of it. The husband, to demonstrate his undying devotion, relinquishes all parts of his single past, including his bank book and cash machine card.

Perhaps it's done this way because the husband feels that he is too busy working and drinking after work with his colleagues to handle the finances. This is the wife's responsibility, which I think she accepts gladly. And why not? She now literally controls the purse strings and becomes chief financial-officer of their household. She uses the money to cover all living expenses and then gives her husband an allowance, from which he can spend as he sees fit on soda pop and candy. Kind of like pin or tuck money, if you will.

I've heard many a man say that he's never had so much pocket money simply because it's better managed. Fairly, I have also heard many grumblings to the contrary.

Yielding one's entire paycheck over for the spouse to use at her discretion is a practice that I doubt will readily become the norm in North America. In Japan it is. Perhaps it is precisely when he's out drinking with the boys, that she goes out and buys the twin beds.

I don't think I'm going out on a limb here, when I propose that on a global scale, men in general appear to get the better deal. On numerous occasions male friends have told me they wanted to get married for one of two reasons. One, they wanted to have someone cook and clean house for them. The other, to produce progeny.

Once I asked a group of female students why they would want to get married. They all answered they wanted to share their life with someone. No one mentioned that they couldn't wait to quit the glamorous photocopying business. But when I asked them why they thought men wanted to get married, they all answered without hesitating that men got married to have children. It was an understanding that seemed acceptable to both parties. Not the most romantic of reasons, but surely practical ones.

The Company Uniform

As with almost all organizations in Japan, be it a school, a company (some head offices excluded), or even a weekend car-driving club, a uniform is perhaps the most fundamental piece of equipment.

Uniforms are introduced in kindergarten and are worn right to the grave. Not the same one all those years mind you, but a uniform of some kind or another. Granted, wearing uniforms can get a little boring, but it saves you a heck of a lot of time deciding what to wear.

"Hmmm... should I wear my blue uniform, or ... my blue uniform?"

On your own time, the sky's the limit, but on company or school time, you wear what you're given and you like it.

Some schools offer trendier uniforms than the traditional navy-blue sailor suit with large collar and skirt, with white socks and penny loafers. This is the girls' uniform by the way. In offering a more up-scale uniform, the school hopes to attract more elite students. Not so long ago, the news reported that a well known bank commissioned a famous designer to produce their new teller's uniforms in hopes of luring 'more attractive' applicants to work at their bank. For one of the most label-conscious nations of consumers in the world, this ploy was quite successful and they were soon turning away pretty, young applicants in droves.

The company I work for quite obviously skimped on design costs. It is my feeling that the company president has always secretly dreamed of being a gas-station attendant. Perhaps he thought it would be a real hoot to fashion the men's uniforms after a 1950s Exxon gas station attendant. Every time I wear it, I have the urge to check oil and clean windshields in the company's parking lot. On a more positive note, the cornflower-blue shirt does bring out the blue in my eyes. As for the other 15,000 employees with brown eyes ...

The origin of the women's uniform leaves less to the imagination. One gets the impression of a school of budding artists as they all wear polyester blue and white checkered smocks.

The company has two uniforms. One for summer and one for winter. I've always been a 'summer' myself. The winter uniform is the gas-pump-attendant number referred to: a utility-style jacket complete with a matching blue cap and pants. The cap, I was told, is for 'safety reasons.' Hmm. That soft blue cotton must have some kind of iron/kevlar weave. Yet, due to my Occidental standing, I don't have to wear the pants. Well, I have to wear pants, just not the company blue ones.

The summer uniform on the other hand is fashioned after a U.S. military shirt. A collared shirt that only buttons up three quarters of the way, with a white T-shirt worn underneath. Instead of saying "Check your oil?" as with the winter uniform, I find myself snapping smart salutes at management personnel.

The company manual of rules and regulations, which is about the size of a car manual, includes detailed instructions on how to properly wear your uniform. It should be pressed and the zipper of the jacket must be level with the line of your top breast pocket. However, while not in the manual, the dates on which you are to switch from summer to winter and back, was understood by all except yours truly.

Much in the same way a bee instinctively knows its way

home, so too do the people of my company know when to change their uniforms. You may think that it would be obvious. When it's too hot or cold you change. But things aren't always what they appear.

You must appreciate that Japan has four distinct seasons. Longitudingly speaking, it runs pretty much from the state of Maine, to the top of Florida. The climate is more or less what you'd find on that stretch of the northeastern U.S. seaboard. However, spring does come fairly early and by the end of May the temperature is reaching into the low thirties (°C). The magical date for switching the winter for the summer uniforms is June 5th. With temperatures as hot as they are at that time of year, I'm sure you'll agree that this date could have been better chosen. I, however, not being from around here, was oblivious to the changing date, and relied on the old, "I'm hot so I'm going change" system. But that was just me.

I relay to you now, almost verbatim, the following conversation which took place in my classroom one hot day in May before all the students arrived for their class.

It was hot. Everyone moved and sweated around the factory like sumo wrestlers, and they sweat profusely, let me tell you. To make things just that much more pleasurable, the air conditioning in my class kept shutting down. The blinking red light indicated that the filter, which I had just removed and cleaned, was indeed still dirty. I eventually turned it off in frustration and sat there to steep in my own juices (eee-yew) with the occasional puff of wind from my one electric fan.

Enter Yukio. A thin 'drink of water' as my grandmother would say, who could never seem to bring himself to look me in the eyes. He panicked momentarily as he noticed that he was the first and only student. As he was an incredibly nervous sort at the best of times, I got the feeling that any sudden movements on my part would cause him to let loose of all his bodily fluids and drop into an unconscious heap on the floor.

I have that effect on people. He was, as I was, sweating quite profusely.

"Hello Mr. Erik."

"Hi Yukio! Hot today isn't it?"

"Yes."

"You should change your winter uniform for your summer one."

"Oh. I can't."

"Why not?"

"Change is June 5th"

"But some people have changed already."

"Yes."

"So … why don't you change?"

"Can't. Change is June 5."

"Is this a company rule?"

"No."

"Is it a rule in your department?"

"No."

"Would your manager get angry if you did?"

"Oh no! Not angry."

The confusing nature of his reluctance to change, coupled with the heat, was starting to irritate me. My not being able to understand why he couldn't change his uniform until the 5th, was irritating him.

"Soooo … why … don't … you … change?"

"Can't. June 5 everybody change."

"But you just said it wasn't a company rule?"

"Yes."

"… and your manager wouldn't mind if you changed before?"

"Yes."

"… and some people have indeed already changed …?"

"Yes."

"… and you're really hot … right?"

"Yes, very."

"So why the hell don't you change!"

"Can't! Must wait for June 5th!"

A silent pause only broken by the sound of the inadequate fan.

"I ... see ...."

At that juncture in our conversation, there was nothing to be done but look at each other, blinking the sweat out of our eyes. The key is knowing when to get out of such a discussion. I have yet to master this. The harder trick is knowing how not to get into such a conversation in the first place. As for the company uniform, common sense in Western culture would dictate that one would change their attire when the temperature allowed, given there would be no repercussions in doing so. Eastern philosophy, tells you to keep the hot one on, and sweat it out with the rest of the gang until June 5th, a date probably intentionally picked by the president to see just who would not toe the company line.

Kacho: "Where's Yamamoto?"

Employee: "He had to go to the infirmary. He got dehydrated."

Kacho: "Now *that's* a company man!"

The only explanation I've received for this apparent act of masochism and other quandaries is, "You're not Japanese, so you wouldn't understand." I guess I'm not.

I guess I don't.

Unions: Are They Worth the Fifty Bucks a Month?

For me, the fifty dollars a month Japanese employees spend on their union dues could be better spent. Now, I will say again, I am in no way an expert in the matters of industrial relations in North America, Asia, or any other continent for that matter. By using the union system at my factory as an example, I'll explain what I mean.

The idea of having a union to protect workers' rights is a good thing. I think we can all agree with that. The union is there to file grievances, offer a variety of services to its members, like insurance etc., and if it should come to that during wage negotiations, strike. Seems like a pretty universal ideology. But how much muscle does the union have when push comes to shove?

The factory union head gets his full-time staff by recruiting members from the factory to take two-year stints as full-time employees in the union office. It can provide a good opportunity for a few young employees to hob-nob with some of the bigger fish in the factory, particularly during negotiation season each spring. Older employees get to play a little of the power game, getting to vent some spleen to management. Kick some butt as it were. The only problem is, after a two-year tenure in the union office is up, they return to their old section and manager, whose butt they quite enjoyably kicked during the last two wage negotiations. Now you tell me: Do you think the manager is going to let bygones be bygones? Somehow, I don't think so. Managers, like elephants, never forget.

"Okay. Let's get down to business. We can't possibly offer a six percent raise. You'll have to settle for two and a third."

"Are you out of your mind! I can't go back to my people with that. Cut me some slack will you?"

"Two and third. Take it or leave it."

"Who do you think you're fooling with here? If you don't come up with the six and a half, we're gonna walk!"

"You can walk all you want to, Yamamoto, but in six months you'll be walking back to our section and after that, your ass is mine."

"Ohhh kay then. I think two and a third is do-able. Can I get anyone more tea?"

This style of system kind of takes the bite out of any union, I think, unless the people they choose are independently wealthy. Given that the union usually accepts any offer after a little dancing around, its function in my mind, is questionable. But then again, I'm not Japanese, so I wouldn't understand.

The Meishi

The business card or *meishi* is one of the most important forms of identification in Japan. It gives that all-important company name and number, as well as the less important personal name.

Unlike North American business cards, the *meishi* is a valued extension of the person giving it. Much as technologically primitive peoples may have thought a photo trapped their soul, so too do the Japanese feel that the *meishi* represents part of their being. What I mean is, if you accepted a Japanese person's business card and promptly put it in your wallet, and then replaced it in your jacket pocket, or heaven forbid, your back pocket, you in essence would be seen as sitting on the soul of your business counterpart with your buttocks. Not a good way to begin negotiations.

If someone presents you with a business card, you are to keep it in front of you on the table to be admired (this also serves a dual purpose of helping you to remember someone's name or as a coaster for a very small glass). Only when the meeting has been officially concluded, and the guest departed, should you put it away.

However, receiving a *meishi* in the first place requires a little delicacy. It is good to remember, that a card is given and received with two hands. Therefore, at one point in the presentation, a total of four hands (four sets of finger-tips) are holding onto a piece of paper the size of a, well, a business card, at the same time. Also, a bow accompanies the handing over of the card. This bow is your standard 45-degree-from-the-hip job. The same rules apply for bowing as previously mentioned in the freshman training section.

The combination of bowing and handing over of the *meishi* is a difficult task requiring some finesse. Not only does one have to be concerned with the appropriate angle of the bow, but also the duration. Unlike the in-house company bow, bowing to someone from a different company follows different guidelines.

In general, I have observed that if it's a 'free style' bow, with no contact point between the people, (no *meishi*) and the bower has his or her hands at their sides, then the underling holds his bow deeper and longer than the person of higher status. Much as a corporal in the army would salute a passing general. The corporal holds his salute until the general has passed, left the building, and has finished his second drink in the Officer's Mess. The general on the other hand just nonchalantly flicks his hand up in acknowledgment on his way by.

A problem that arises when presenting a *meishi* to a superior and bowing at the same time is "Whose duration of bow-time do you use?" I mean, the President of Toyota Motors isn't going to get down and bow the same length of time when meeting the 'Employee of the Decade' from the shop floor. Reciprocally, the working man wouldn't dare bow for any lesser time than was required in such a situation. Hence, the *meishi* is left held aloft for a few seconds and is taken only at the last moment by the superior.

For people of the same station, it can be just as nerve-wracking. It's like handshaking. You don't want to let go too early and make the other person feel like they've got some kind of highly communicable disease. Nor do you want to hold on too long. The other person gives your hand a hearty shake, and lets go. You're still smiling and holding on. The next thing you know, you're being asked out for dinner and dancing after the meeting.

In the same light, you can't let go of your *meishi* before the other guy's got a hold of it, causing it to fall to the floor, nor do you want to be hauled off balance if you don't let go. Timing is the key, which only comes with practice.

Over the past few decades, another twist has been added to this delicate art. With the introduction of Western style business practices, the handshake has also been incorporated into this ritualistic dance.

When two Japanese salarymen (regular company business men) meet, the *meishi* is brought out simultaneously by both parties. As they are going down into the bow, the *meishi* is held by both hands out front and a little lower than waist level. With the hands and arms locked into this position, they bow a few times. Once that is completed, the card is brought forward in a gentle upward sweeping motion, bringing the hands up towards the face, as the body remains fixed in the position of the last bow. Just before (this is the tricky part), the hands reach the apex of the swing, the left hand freezes into position while holding the *meishi*. The right hand, having let go, continues a bit more to the top of the arc and clasps hands with his counterpart, forming an 'X' pattern with the forearms. At this point, both parties shake, bow a little more, and release their respective cards to end in an upright position, all at the same time, the swap having been completed.

Poetry in motion.

A quick glance at the card verifies that you did indeed end up with your partner's card and not your own.

Those unpracticed end up looking like grown men in suits doing an impression of two lumber-jacks sawing logs. Not a good first impression.

On one occasion I ran out of business cards and needed to have more printed up. I never really get that much of an opportunity to hand them out over here, but they're good party favours in my home town, as they are written in English on one side and Japanese on the other. The printer inevitably makes spelling errors in English which is good for a few laughs.

On this day, I took two cards over to my section to use as samples for the printer. On one, I used liquid paper to white-out my English title of 'English Language and Cultural Instructor.' In its place I had printed, 'Master of Time, Space and Dimension.' I explained to the person in charge of these matters that the 'new' English version was a little more meaningful to foreign visitors (i.e. my friends at home). The Japanese version would remain the same. She smiled and took the samples.

By the time I had returned to my classroom located in a different building in the factory compound, the young woman had obviously been thumbing through her Japanese-English dictionary and called me to confirm the meaning of my new title.

"It means ... I'm a 'Jack-of-All-Trades'"

"You ... are 'Jack Off' what?"

"No, no, not 'Jack Off', but 'Jack-of', one 'F'. 'Jack-of-All-Trades.'"

"Eh?"

"It means I do many different things around the factory in English, not just teaching. I write letters, check papers, that kind of thing."

"Ahhh so ka. I understand. Thank you. Bye bye." She hung up.

"Yes!"

However, my little ruse didn't last long. A short while later, the phone rang with my manager at the other end, whose English language ability probably surpasses my own in many ways.

"Erik. Are you busy? Can you spare a moment?"

"Certainly. How can I help you?"

"It's in regards to your business cards. I have your sample in front of me. I was wondering if you could explain to me the meaning of this Master of Time and something or other?"

"Of course. It means that I do many functions in English

for many different sections in the factory." I swallowed hard and hoped he couldn't hear it. I didn't know what kind of punishment they would inflict on someone for tampering with the company's *meishi*. I'd probably be a test case, and it might even go to trial.

"Ah so ka. So what I guess you're telling me is that you don't really need them ... do you?"

The dreaded rhetorical question.

"No sir. The originals will do just fine. Thank you."

"I thought so. Good-bye Mr. Gingles."

"Good-bye."

That's why he's the manager.

Holidays and Festivals

Adopted Holidays (Part One): Halloween and Christmas

In Japan, there are holidays, Western in origin, that are gaining widespread popularity. Primarily, as it's been said to me, the Japanese love a festival. It doesn't matter what the basis of it is, so long as it's got a track record of fun, and businesses can make some money at it.

Take Halloween. It's becoming more popular every year, but no one can tell you the origin of the event. Near the end of October stores are filled with ghosts and goblins and plastic pumpkins filled with candy. I asked a student why they thought the pumpkin was a symbol of Halloween. The answer: "Because the pumpkin looks pretty." Granted, this particular pumpkin did look rather cute, but that's not the point. Foreign traditions are introduced into a host culture, but their origins are rarely explained. This could not be more true than when talking about Christmas.

Many Asian countries celebrate the birth of Christ with verve and splendour, since they, unlike Japan, have a substantial Christian base to work with.

Every year, we see more and more Christmas lights go up downtown. More and more decorations fill the malls and Christmas Muzak fills the air as parents try to choose just the right gift. There's that ole familiar feeling of spending in the air.

All of this has happened fairly recently, given Christmas' two-thousand-year history. Ten years ago, young men would perhaps take their sweetie out for Christmas Eve dinner at a nice restaurant. Occasionally, a gift might be exchanged. Families on the other hand, would eat Christmas cake on the 24th. Not your typical fruitcake, but a two- or three-layered, white-icing job with chocolate reindeer and Santas doing laps around the traditional Christmas strawberries. These cakes have become big business. The 7-11's, which number in the kazillions, produce a cake catalog and store owners urge their customers to place an order for their cake before time runs out. The owner of the 7-11 near our house seemed most distressed two years ago that we would be without the traditional Christmas cake on Christmas Eve. After all, it was 'our' tradition. I thanked him for his concern, but assured him we would make do, and the Christmas spirit would live on.

Going from a fruitcake to a fluffy white cake with Santas is not much of a deviation. However it seems a bit much when a local mall portrayed the Nativity scene using Santa's elves instead of Wise Men, and a huge plastic slice of Christmas cake as the centre piece.

Kentucky Fried Chicken have added their bit and portray the traditional Christmas meal as being a bucket of their best. The image on posters and television would have you believe, that, from the dawn of time, mothers would spend the day, not slaving away in the kitchen, but standing in line at the closest KFC to pick up that once in a year and long awaited traditional Christmas pack.

"Well, there you go. I hope you like it. "

"Thank your mother, boys."

"Thank you, Ma'am."

"Thank you, Ma'am."

"Mmmmm good, Hon! You know, boys, you're lucky. Nobody, and I do mean nobody picks up KFC like your mom."

"Oh Ed! Stop it. You're embarrassing me."

This particular portrayal of Christmas by KFC (or me) is

not so much of a misunderstanding of the tradition, but more of a company's merely trying to form the general public's perception of Christmas to their benefit. You can't really blame them for that. It's their job and it's a universal thing. However, occasionally a company bites off a bit more than it can chew, causing signals to get crossed.

I experienced this same kind of phenomenon a long time ago in university. I had to read more novels than humanly possible in order to graduate with my English major. Well … it would have been a little more humane if I had done the readings when they were assigned, but that's not the point. The point is, that after all that continuous reading, the stories in the novels kind of merged into one. I soon found I couldn't distinguish between them. They all seemed to be about the Prince of Denmark who was seeking his father's revenge by hunting down this great white whale called 'Moby something-or-other' who had this scarlet letter somehow tattooed on its belly which he wore as a badge of courage.

Without guidance, the mixing of Christian/Christmas stories and their symbols can happen in the same manner. A Japanese English magazine reported one classic incident of misrepresentation. It seems that a large store of a huge department store chain in Tokyo had hanging outside, and all lit up for the buying public to see, a twenty-foot smiling Santa … nailed to a cross.

Let's not panic. Maybe there's deeper symbolism here than we're giving the department store PR guys credit for. Maybe the cross represents the cross we, as consumers of Christmas gifts, all bear. The cross is the burden, if you will, of finding the appropriate gift for the right person. Santa, therefore, could be the embodiment of all consumers, as we are the real gift givers. Santa is therefore 'nailed' to his great responsibilities much in the same way we are nailed to the burden of actually buying the gifts. Why Santa is smiling is a little harder to explain. Perhaps that's the true brainchild of the department store. Maybe he's smiling because he's going to get all of his

Christmas shopping done this year, under one roof, in this one store. But I doubt it.

Realistically, this befuddled image of Christmas was the result of no one in the promotions department bothering to check out the legitimacy of their idea. It was probably a bunch of guys sitting around the coffee machine trying to come up with some new gimmick. Besides, who's gonna know the difference?

"So, what about this Santa idea of mine? You know, putting him outside for the Christmas sales. Cream?"

"Thanks. And what are we supposed to hang him on?" (slurp)

"How about nailing him to that cross he carries around?"

"Yeah. That'd work. Sushi tonight?"

I have no documents to substantiate this conversation and will deny having written it if questioned, but how else could you explain a department store nailing a smiling Santa to a cross and hoisting him up for all to see?

And so this is Christmas.

Cherry Blossom Parties (a.k.a. Alcohol Poisoning)

The Cherry Blossom is one of the most recognized symbols of Japan. The entire country is formally introduced to Spring by a two-week period in which the cherry trees bloom. At the end of every evening TV newscast, a map follows the progress of the blossoms across the country. They start opening in the south and work their way north, like a huge wave of white and pink blanketing the country. River banks, parks and mountainsides come alive with this spectacular show of natural beauty. Yet, as gently and as quickly they come, likewise they go. The trees shower admirers under their boughs with a flurry of delicate pink petals as they near the end of their cycle.

It's a short two weeks from the time of the first bloom to the falling of the first petal. Family and friends gather under the trees to celebrate this glorious event. And what better way to heighten your senses and appreciation of such a natural wonder, than through complete and utter alcohol inebriation.

All across the land, people have 'Cherry Blossom Viewing Parties' — *hanami* in Japanese. Almost every group or committee you may belong to has one. It's usually a barbecue party held under some cherry trees. Everyone sits on blue plastic ground sheets, and then drinks beer and sake until they fall over stinking drunk or go temporarily blind.

Every city has different areas where the trees can be found in abundance. For us in Matsumoto, the two places most visited for such parties are along the main riverbank in town, a seven-hundred-year-old burial mound that is completely covered with cherry trees and looks very much like a huge pile of cotton candy, and the castle with its surrounding park.

During this festive time, the castle and its moat can be too much of a temptation for some. At the height of revelry last year, six university students ripped off their clothes and decided to jump naked into the water, much to the surprise and displeasure of the carp and swans living therein.

Caroline and I prefer the sights at the burial mound. It has a path that snakes its way to the top and is lit with paper lanterns creating a pink tunnel of petals for the duration of the blossoming. Every year we take a picnic and head up the hill. Avoiding the crowds and drunken mayhem at the top, we slip off the main path to a little private clearing where we can set up camp for a few hours in our own dimly lit pink cave. It's enchanting to sit there, slowly sipping wine and eating dinner. Enveloped by the soft light of the paper lanterns illuminating our lair, we can listen to the distant merry-makers above.

Ahhh, this is the life. However, one must be careful not to stray too far from the path. The public toilets, like garbage cans, are few and far between. The area surrounding these prime spots soon becomes one great big outhouse for all forms of bodily expulsions. Maybe that's why everyone sits on the blue plastic ground sheets.

As far as the riverbank goes, it probably gets the most visitors due to its size and length. There's not a whole lot of actual blossom-viewing going on there, as the best flat space to set up for a barbecue is a bit further down the river, away from the cherry trees. But that's a moot point. On the weekends, people will go early in the morning and pin down their blue plastic sheet to reserve a spot, then come back later in the afternoon to get things rolling. It's almost one continuous line of ground sheets for 300 metres, filled with barbecues, Coleman lanterns, bonfires, fireworks and lots and lots of beer. The only thing really missing is the cherry blossoms. But like I said, that's a moot point.

And so, after a two-week period of festive merry-making, the petals fall, and the blue plastic sheets are sadly put away until next time. The season is short, but nature knows best. No one's body (or liver) could withstand anything longer.

National Holidays

Note: This chapter is minorly statistical and can be skipped unless you've got a hankering to know about Japan's national holidays or think it might be a Jeopardy question.

From my place of employ, I get a total of fifty, count 'em, fifty days paid holiday in one working year. Fifty days! (gloat gloat). Twenty-one days are personal holidays to use at my discretion, and the other twenty-nine are national or company holidays. In regards to the national holidays, at least three times a year the entire country is off for a week. What a mess on the highway that makes.

The first of these week-long holidays comes at the tail end of December and the first week of January. New Year is traditionally one of the big family times. Everyone goes to the temple and prays for the things they hope to have happen in the coming year. Passing grades in school, better health, or a new car with a remote CD player. At the temples, the staff (high school students who do this as a part-time job instead of bagging groceries) sell good-luck arrows and other doodads to ward off evil spirits from entering your house during the coming year. These talismans are hung over your door and act like an evil-spirit filter. By the end of the year, the filters are full and have to be replaced. Hence, at the temples where you can buy them, there are usually large bonfires that you throw your saturated evil-spirit filter into. Next, you spend $20 to get a new one.

When it comes to praying for something, money talks. A person can buy a small, special wooden plaque that resembles the front view of a house. With a marker, you write your wish on the front. These plaques are then hung up all over big bulletin boards around the temple grounds. The amount you pay determines just how far up the request line you get. If your wish isn't answered that year, what recourse do you have?

"Hey! I came here last year and paid $100 to get a promotion and it didn't happen."

"A hundred dollars for a promotion? Oh dear. Promotions usually run at least three hundred. Tell you what. You give me $250 and I'll see what I can do."

The rest of the calendar's holidays go a little something like this:

January 15th. — *Seijin-no hi* — Coming of Age Day. — Honouring all those who've reached the legal age of twenty from the previous April to the current year's April. A huge public ceremony is held and all the qualifying young adults dress in their coming-of-age best (kimono or suit), get together for a big photo, and then head home for a celebratory dinner with family and friends. Of course, in my hometown, the only photo taken on that day would be for a liquor licence.

February 11th. — *Kenkoku hinen-no hi* — National Foundation Day. Celebrating the coronation of the first recognized emperor some 2000 years ago. But who's counting?

March 21st — *Shumbun-no hi* — Vernal Equinox. — Sounds a bit pagan, but on this day of the spring equinox, families gather and visit the graves of relatives.

The next few days are strung together during the last week

of April and the first week of May. It's referred to as 'Golden Week.' Many companies will tack on a few days to make the week complete, thereby forming the second week-long holiday of the year.

April 29th — *Midori-no hi* — Greenery Day. — (if you haven't figured it out yet, 'Hi,' pronounced, 'hee' means 'Day'). This is a bit of a stretch, but it's a national holiday to appreciate ... greenery. Originally it was Emperor Hirohito's birthday, but since his death in the eighties and the debates as to the level of his involvement in the last world war, celebrating his birthday wasn't as politically correct as it used to be. As not long ago he was considered a living god, wiping it off the calendar was a bit blasphemous, so they changed the name, but kept the date.

May 3rd — *Kempo Kinenbi* — Constitution Day. — Commemorates Japan's new way of government. In 1947 Japan devised a new democratic constitution based on the American Constitution.

May 5th — *Kodomo-no hi* — Children's Day. — My mother used to claim, whenever I asked her on Mother's Day why there wasn't a Kids Day, that "Every day was 'Kids Day.'" What a scam. Here, it's a nationally recognized holiday and a day off.

September 15th — *Keiro-no hi* — Respect for the Aged Day. — A day to reflect on just how old Grams and Gramps really are. It's a good thing for the families to be kind to their elders, as they usually hold the deeds to the house you and your family are living in, that's been passed down from generation to generation.

September 23rd — *Shubun-no hi* — Autumn Equinox. — Another grave-site visiting day to pay continued respects to the spirits of ancestors.

October 10th — Taiku-no hi — Sports Day. — No, this is not a sister city sports challenge. It's a day to commemorate the opening of the 1964 Tokyo Olympics. If that's worth a holiday, then one year after the Winter Olympics in 1998, I'd expect you'll see a 'Winter Sports Day' gracing the 1999 calendar.

November 3rd — *Bunkai-no hi* — Culture Day. — On this day, no one, and I mean NO ONE, is allowed to pick their nose, or eat with their elbows on the table. Just kidding. It's really a day to reflect on the good life. All over the city you can watch demonstrations of countless traditional Japanese arts. While the younger boys are in the parks displaying various forms of kicking each other or hitting each other with bamboo sticks, women, dressed in resplendent kimonos. are showing the more genteel arts of flower arranging and tea ceremony.

November 23rd — *Kinro-no hi* — Labour Day. — Much as in North America, it's a long weekend without much ceremony. Local union offices put on marching (shuffling) parades on the main streets holding their particular union banner in front of them, saying something indistinguishable, even to the Japanese, into a crackly bullhorn.

December 23rd — *Tenno Tanjobi* — Emperor's Birthday. — As just one emperor before was considered a true living god, it seems only fitting that his son's birthday (the current, and only emperor in the world) is taken as a national holiday. That close to Christmas, I wonder if he gets two gifts, or a combined gift?

If you add these days up, you'll notice that the total is not the fifty that I mentioned earlier. The company I work for provides a gaggle more on top of what's mentioned above. Many smaller companies however, still have a six day-work-week, or at best, have every second Saturday off. The younger generation however, appear to be evolving into the 'me generation' and are more interested in their own pursuits and enjoyment of life.

A newspaper article stated that as a result of this pursuit of happiness, university graduates are starting to choose companies that offer more holiday time over a higher paying salary.

Kids today.

Adopted Holidays (Part Two): Valentine's Day and White (Panty) Day

Unlike Christmas, Valentine's Day is a custom that has far less wires to be crossed. But as stated earlier, things of a foreign origin are altered somewhat when assimilated into a different culture. Even simple things. In Japan there are some fast food restaurants that put fried eggs on their cheeseburgers. Likewise, Valentine's Day is slightly modified. I'm not suggesting that they give their sweethearts chocolate-covered fried eggs, but it's the women who give the chocolates to the men. The men are the receivers. The woman the givers. Sounds pretty good to me.

I was rather flattered on my first Valentine's Day in Japan. After having received a very respectable amount of chocolate, I was feeling quite the man about the factory (B.M.O.F.) My bubble wasn't long inflated as I soon discovered that most Valentine's Day chocolate is referred to as *Giri Choco* — loosely translated means 'Obligation Chocolate.' As the name implies, it's not given out of affection. Because they work with you and you are part of the team, women co-workers feel obligated to give you chocolate. I was crushed. But ever the optimist, I had to wonder to myself, "Why did they feel obligated to me? And just how could this obligation be repaid? Hmm?" Anyway. It's kind of like drawing names at the office to choose a 'Secret Santa.' You pick a name(s), and that's who you're obligated to buy for. Apparently, some big department stores (they always come up with the good ideas) sell *Giri Choco* Paks, which have different size sets of chocolates. Larger ones for the general manager, a smaller one for the section manager and so on down the line. How sweet love is.

Valentine's Day however, is not as one-sided as it first appears. On March 14th, exactly one month after Valentine's Day, the men who received chocolate, have to return the favour. This day is called 'White Day.' As for the meaning, no one I've asked can give me an explanation. And on White Day, men give … cookies.

You see, basically (very basically), a large Japanese cookie manufacturer was getting a little miffed that his counterpart chocolate manufacturer buddy was cashing in on this Western tradition of Valentine's Day. The general public was hungry for anything Western in culture. He had to get his cookies to the people. So, using Valentine's Day as a stepping stone, he and his cookie compadres started promoting the fictional 'White Day' in conjunction with the chocolate-giving custom. Voila! A new tradition was born.

To take this a step farther, another manufacturer started to get into the act and latched onto White Day. Though not as traditional, it's interesting to say the least. And how their marketing guys convinced the public this was the way it's done and accepted in North America, I'll never know, but they had to be very good to pull it off.

On White Day I asked one of my female students at break time how many boxes of cookies she received. Her answer was a little more than I bargained for.

"I got three boxes of cookies, and two pairs of panties."

"What? Who gave you the panties?"

She seemed a little surprised at my reaction.

"The Assistant Manager did. Why?"

I couldn't believe it. Her Assistant Manager? I thought he was married.

"Really? Did he say anything to you?"

"He said 'Here, these are for you.'"

"That's it?"

"Of course. What else should he say?"

I had a hard time trying to put into perspective how this young, usually shy girl, had such an open attitude about undergarments given to her by an assistant manager.

"What should he say? What should he say? I don't know, maybe, 'How about a drink after work?' or something like that."

"A drink after work with … him?" She seemed a bit repulsed by the idea.

"Well. I just figured that if the guy is giving you underpants at the office, there must be something between you two."

"Between us!" Now she was looking around to see if anyone was really paying attention, which admittedly they usually aren't in class.

"What gave you that idea?"

Now I was really confused. It seemed obvious to me that only people of an intimate nature go around giving each other underpants, unless of course it's your mom.

"Well, maybe it's because he's giving you underpants instead of cookies?"

"So? He gave underpants to all the girls in the section. And besides, his wife probably bought them."

Now I'm thinking that's a pretty open relationship. He makes the money, and his wife buys the panties for his girls.

"Are you kidding me? His wife bought them? Is that normal?"

"I don't think so."

Finally. We were getting on the same wavelength.

"If I was his wife, I'd make him get his own panties. I wouldn't be his slave."

Oy Veh. I was obviously missing something.

"You mean that it's okay for a married man to give another woman panties in his office?"

"Sure. Why not? It's for White Day. It doesn't mean anything. Didn't you know that?"

My silence and look of comprehension answered for me. "Ohhhh ... you mean they don't give panties on White Day in North America?"

I pity the man from Japan who gets transferred to North America around Valentine's Day. He's in for a rude awakening with something called sexual harassment.

"Ah, Miss Johnson. Thank you so much for your giving of me the chocolates. Now I have special White Day gift for you. I bet I surprise you "

"A... White Day present? And for me? Oh Mr. Yamamoto, you shouldn't have. That's so sweet."

Mr. Yamamoto would probably be looking over her shoulder, wondering what colour his wife bought.

"What the hell...."

WHAM! before Mr. Yamamoto knows what's happened, he's out cold, and by the time he wakes up, he's on the slow boat back to Japan with a big ole 'Undesirable' stamp in his passport. Hence, my business card says, 'English Language and Cultural Instructor.'

White Day in North America. Ha! Good luck.

Love

The Business of Love

Love and romance sells. Economies all over the world are bolstered by gifts to a loved one. From a simple card to the Taj Mahal. In Japan, geological/socio-economic differences spur on another huge money-maker for the economy.

The catalyst of this particular industry is lack of space. Simply put, there just isn't enough private space to get to know someone on a more personal level. Everyone usually has three or four generations living under the same roof, so it's difficult to find the house empty with just you and your romantic interest. Even if your parents went out for the evening, you'd be financially hard pressed to send the rest of the clan to the movies for the night.

With the house out of bounds, the next private place might be your car. Besides the physical limitations of entertaining in a car, there are very few truly private places to park. Everywhere you go is somewhere, and at somewhere is always someone. So where do the lovelorn go?

Enter Love Hotels. Perhaps you've heard of them? They are hotels for romantic to sadomasochistic encounters. And they make a fortune. So much so, that a semi-conductor engineer who's not prone to exaggeration, said that he read in a trade magazine (semi-conductor that is) that the amount of money love hotels pull in exceeds the total amount of the entire semi-conductor industry in Japan! That's a whole lotta lovin' going on.

For the most part, they don't look like regular hotels or motels. Some resemble office buildings, while others go for the flash of a Las Vegas casino. The entrances are off the main road and lovers enter by car through a small opening in a surrounding wall. Some hotels offer individual parking garages for each room. If you haven't guessed by now, these precautions are to help ensure privacy for the hotel's guests. Some of the cheaper hotels don't have the individual garages, so they provide wooden stands about three feet high in the shape of a heart to place in front of your rear licence plate.

The 'secrecy act' doesn't end with your car. There is no one at the front desk. In fact, there rarely is a front desk. The lobby is accessed from the private door of your own garage. Here you will find a display board on the wall with back-lit pictures of all the rooms. If there's no red light next to a picture, then that room is vacant. Most are theme rooms of sorts. There's the Cowboy room with bucking bronco, leather straps, and stuff. The Ship's Captain's room is decorated in dark wood and the walls are made to look like the inside of a Spanish galleon. And for the brave of heart, there's an S and M room complete with cave-like walls that have working shackles attached. Whips and chains are strategically placed around the room.

After you've decided on a room, all you have to do to get your key is to press the corresponding button to your room on the 'Room Vending Machine,' and your key drops out. From there a couple can head up to their room via an elevator which is built for two people. The hallways are dark and eerily quiet. Dim lights recessed in the ceiling help you to find your room number. Once inside, the door locks behind you and cannot be opened, even from the inside, until your time is up. And that's all I'm going to say. The rest is up to you.

I have insider knowledge from the simple fact that, well,

I went there. For Caroline's birthday actually. I can't really say if it was more for me or for her, but we did. It was really quite nice. The room was lavishly appointed and about twice the size of our apartment with a huge Jacuzzi to boot.

I was all set to go when Caroline got home that evening after work. I told her we were going somewhere for the rest of the night and to bring her cowboy boots. Just kidding.

Once in the car, I asked her to use the bandanna I brought to blindfold herself as the location of where we were going was a surprise. The hotel I had in mind meant we had to get on the express toll-highway for about fifteen kilometres. Caroline was confused to say the least in regards to our destination, but no more surprised than the old guy working the toll gate. When I pulled up to his window, he looked in to see two foreigners. One, a male sheepishly handing him some money and the other, a female, wearing a blindfold.

"It's her birthday."

It didn't help.

We were soon in the parking lot of the hotel and circling the building like a passenger plane waiting its turn at a busy airport. I was trying to locate a vacant garage. Caroline announced she was getting woozy. I asked her to hold on as we were almost there. Who would have thought that there would be so many romantics out on a Tuesday night?

After a few more rounds of the building, an empty garage appeared and we were in. With the blindfold off, and colour returning to her cheeks, Caroline announced,

"We're in the garage of a Love Hotel, aren't we!"

So much for the surprise. Then it dawned on me. Just how did she know what the inside of love-hotel parking garage looked like?

Once in the lobby, we made our room selection (heh heh) and then had to decide between two options. We could have the two-hour 'Rest' and pay sixty dollars or choose the twelve-hour 'Stay' and pay one hundred and ten. I figured twelve hours was a bit optimistic, so I selected the two-hour option.

Up the elevator we went.

By the time we got to the room, figured out what all the buttons on the wall panel did, and got the Jacuzzi filled, the two hours were pretty much up. I got on the phone to the phantom lobby and said in Neanderthal Japanese. "Room good. I stay."

And that was that.

It was good sleep on a huge bed for a change and in the morning we were treated to a spectacular view of the Northern Alps. The whole east wall was a curved window offering a incredible panorama of the snow-capped mountains. I had a beatific smile on my face. The thought of leaving this massive room and returning to the confines of our apartment was a little disheartening. I was also wondering just how I was supposed to pay.

Picking up the phone, I got a short greeting from the imaginary front desk.

"*Hai.*"

Not knowing what to say in such a situation, and not having the Japanese vocabulary to dance around the issue, I was limited in my response options. "I'm done."

The look on Caroline's faced told me she wasn't pleased with my choice of words.

"*Hai.*"

The line went dead. Now what? Before the receiver was back in its cradle, we could make out a faint rattling sound coming from somewhere in the bowels of the building. Something was approaching our room from the inside and coming quick. It sounded like something caught in a vacuum cleaner. It flew overhead, across the ceiling and stopped with a 'Pthhhhhhh' at a little window unnoticed until now. That's neat. I stood for a second with the phone receiver still in hand before I hung up and went over to the little windowed door in the wall.

Inside was a plastic capsule containing our bill. Just like the old department stores used to have. There was a complete artery system throughout the entire building that vacuumed bills, payment and change to a central cashier. I put in some cash, closed the door and hit a button. 'Whooosh!' Away it went. A few moments later the rattling could be heard approaching again.

'Pthhhhhhh.' Our change was ready and there was an enclosed discount card for our next 'stay.'

Subsequently, my sister sent me an article from her local newspaper, *The Halifax Herald*, that described this wondrous world of love hotels. It stated the needs of these hotels are slowly changing. Only sixty percent of the hotels' business can be attributed to romantic endeavours. Now I'm thinking, "And how do they go about checking that?" Regardless of their means of surveying, they go on to say that twenty-one percent of their customers were young males who (pardon the pun) came by themselves.

Anyway, the thing is, that besides having round beds and the like, these rooms are entertainment centres. They can have Karaoke machines, miniature swimming pools or even a golf-driving range on the balcony. The article went on to say that a lot of young couples don't have any intention of doing anything romantic but are there to use the rooms as a private recreational facility. A young woman was quoted as saying that it was really a bargain considering the price she'd have to pay for a spot on the golf-driving range. Here, she gets one for her own private use and can sing a few songs during a break.

With this market research, the Association of Love Hotel owners are starting to cater to this new platonic clientele. They're promoting some of their hotels as a kind of adult game centre providing privacy and/or a 'Rest' area.

Donkey Kong anyone?

The Business of Weddings

If I could choose any profession in Japan, without a doubt, it would be the wedding business. By this I mean the companies that hold weddings in a 'Wedding Plaza.' They have all the dresses and tuxedos for rent, arrange all the food, drinks, light show, cake, videographer and even a professional M.C. How much money is in this?

Bags.

I clued into the amount of money being made when a young co-worker decided to get married. She was looking through the dress-rental catalog at lunch and couldn't decide which dress she wanted, nor how many. I had to ask.

"What do you mean by 'How many.'"

"Oh … at least three or four."

"Four?"

Apparently that's the norm. The first dress is usually an all-white wedding kimono worn at the temple's private ceremony. The second is a colourful kimono to be worn at the reception. The third follows the second kimono and is a Western-style white wedding dress. Finally, the bride changes for the last time into a ballroom gown to light the candles on the guest's tables with her new hubby, using a three-foot-long butane lighter. Those are just rentals. Then she'll wear her own new outfit for leaving the hotel. Out of habit, I add things like that up in my head.

"It must be kind of expensive."

"Hmmm, a little. Each kimono's rental is about $5000 and the ballroom gown is $4000."

Can you imagine? Over $18,000 U.S. just in dress rentals for one day. Plus you've got his tuxedo rentals, of which only two are needed but at roughly $2000 a pop. All totaled, that's over $22,000 just in clothes rentals! I suggested that for half that she could fly over to Hong Kong for a three-day vacation with her boyfriend Eigi, stay at the posh Peninsula Hotel, get a hand-made wedding dress, and do all kinds of other shopping.

"Hmm. I suppose. But we will rent."

Having too much of my mother in me, I couldn't let it go. "But why?"

"Because it's what everyone does."

How many times have I heard that over the years. Not only was this the reason, but it was a 'keeping up with the Yamamotos' mentality. "Can't let the Yamamotos have a bigger wedding for their daughter than mine. What would the manager think?" I realized with this kind of thinking, you could keep all your TV and stereo companies. Keep the car and semi-conductor companies. Just give me the wedding plazas.

So the usual Japanese wedding is indeed expensive, and quite readily more so than the average North American wedding — particularly in regards to attire. However, these weddings are also a financial burden on the guests. When you are invited to a friend's wedding, only the person whose name appears on the invitation is allowed to attend. There are no guests of a guest. Hence, if my wife receives an invitation, and the couple doesn't know me very well, I'm not invited. Just Caroline. It's not assumed that your spouse, boyfriend or whoever will accompany you. It's a bit of a knock to your ego if you both know a couple but your spouse gets the invitation and you don't. Yet, it can be a blessing in disguise.

As I said, a wedding is expensive for the guests as well. Each person attending is not expected to bring a gift as such, but a cash donation instead. This money is used to help cover the cost of the wedding and to help pay for the gifts you will receive upon the conclusion of the dinner. An average friend is expected to pay around $200 U.S. A closer friend from $250 to $500 U.S. Yikes! No wonder nobody shows any real outward emotion to their friends over here. If you get too chummy with somebody you may get soaked for five hundred bucks when they get married. Not a good idea to be too popular. Financially speaking, your best bet is to keep your acquaintances strictly limited to hamsters or gerbils.

At some time or other, through no fault of your own, you might find that you do indeed have a friend and that you've been invited to their wedding.

This traditional wedding service was established during the Meiji period roughly one hundred years ago. It takes place at a Shinto shrine with a priest. Only the immediate family is allowed to attend. In this ceremony, the important symbolic act of the couple joining as one is not the exchanging of rings, but by the passing of the sake. They perform a ritual called *Sansan kudo* which means 'three-three-nine times.' The bride and groom have three formal sips of sake, gradually going from small cups to larger ones. This was normally carried out only in the high-ranking households. Perhaps, because weddings were arranged from birth back then, they thought it prudent to get the couple a little sauced before they tied the knot with a total stranger. After sealing the bonds of their love with the sake, the whole show moves to a different location for the reception.

As for Yoko's wedding to Eigi, they followed the now traditional path of extravagance.

After they finished the private ceremony in the shrine, which by the way was conveniently located in the wedding plaza, they opted for the 'Western Wedding' package. I don't mean to imply that everyone wore cowboy boots and rode a mechanical bull in the corner. It meant that she wore a Western-style traditional white wedding dress in a simulated church chapel (again conveniently located in the wedding plaza just above the shrine) and an organist played the wedding march.

The chapel was an elongated narrow room with a red carpet down the centre which was covered with a white sheet, allowing the guests to keep their outside shoes on while walking down the aisle. The pews were diminutive and sat five abreast rather uncomfortably, and there were about ten rows on each side. The front of the chapel did have a pulpit on one side with the organist on the other. Everyone looked suitably serious. The 'Wedding March' began and Yoko, dressed in a long white wedding gown, entered from the back with her proud father dressed in a morning coat. Yoko hesitated and seemed a little unsteady. Perhaps she had just a wee too much sake in the first ceremony. Looking down at her feet, I noticed her tentative steps were a result of her shoes. In trying to add a little Western height, she was wearing shoes with six-inch heels, that had five-inch platform soles as well. The sheet on the thick carpet didn't help much either.

The whole ceremony was over in no time and then the hired singers led everyone in a hymn. The first was "What a Friend We Have in Jesus." The second sounded very much like the Russian national anthem. To finish off, the presiding priest (who looked very much like the guy I saw parking cars) said the benediction, and then the newlyweds tottered back down the aisle.

The only snag to the whole event at that point was my fault. Not understanding the announcement at the beginning of the service against taking any pictures, I stepped into the aisle and let loose with a flurry of photos. The flash caused Yoko to waver a bit, but Eigi, ever the gentleman, steadied her and they continued on their way.

Waiting Wedding Plaza staff then whisked the couple off for official photographs. The guests who attended the optional Western wedding now joined the other guests waiting in the lobby of the main hall and probably informed them of the bozo who was taking photos when he shouldn't have. This diversion was probably not appreciated since until the first toast is made at the reception, no one can drink. There are no cocktails beforehand, so any delays in getting to that first toast are most unwelcome. After all, it is $200 a plate.

Finally, the show was about to begin. The crowd filed in past the receiving line to their assigned tables. The seating, as is customary, was done according to association. Co-workers were in one area, high school friends at another, and the parents sat at the very back. The group closest to the head table was comprised of their assistant manager and other business dignitaries or business associates of the bride's father. The head table itself had the couple sitting in the middle and their matchmakers were sitting on either side.

The modern day matchmakers' responsibility is to meet with the couple a few times to make sure that this is what they really want to do. The matchmakers rarely have had anything to do with the couples' first meeting. And if you haven't already guessed, nine times out of ten, the matchmakers are the groom's manager and his wife.

The manager, being the surrogate father, gets to sit at the head table with his wife. She has only met the couple on two previous occasions at best and only then to offer tea. The real parents, on the other hand, who have nurtured them and brought them into this world, get to sit at the back.

So now we're seated. The lights go out as a huge spotlight illuminates the entrance with a dazzling bluish-white light. The Wedding March, this time recorded, fills the room with surround-sound. Through the mist produced by the fog machine located over the door, the couple enters to the applause of their guests. Given the flashy entrance and props, I was almost expecting the groom in his silver tux to pull a rabbit out of his pocket, make his new wife levitate, and then for a grand finale, make her disappear.

Instead, they smiled politely and bowed this way and that

as they made their way to the head table, which was no small feat with a four-million mega-watt spotlight in your face the whole way. It was pretty spectacular to see Yoko all kimono-ed up against the brilliant eight-foot-high accordioned gold backdrop behind the head table that all weddings have.

The hired M.C. stood up and thanked everyone for coming and then called on someone to lead the much awaited first toast. With a droning of words ending with *kampai!* (cheers), the beer and wine began to flow. During the following meal, designated speakers got up to make speeches. Oddly, no one was listening. I mean no one, except for the few sitting right in front of the microphone. People were laughing and talking with their neighbours, making all kinds of noise. Yet somehow on cue, all guests would stop whatever they were doing and clap when the person was finished.

With most weddings, another part of the dinner's entertainment usually involves friends who have been asked to come up with some kind of skit to perform. If it's women, they usually sing some song the bride likes and let it go at that. Men tend to get into lame skits full of personal jokes that none of the guests get, sometimes not even the groom.

True to form, Eigi's co-workers performed a skit that was fashioned after a TV game show. The groom wore a kid's bicycle helmet with a flashing light (like a police car) attached to the top. He was then asked a series of questions. If he answered incorrectly, as determined by the quiz master, the red light on his head would come on. It had potential, but I'll leave it up to you if they hit the mark or not. The Quiz Master began.

"Okay everyone! We're now going to ask Eigi a few questions and see if he's telling the truth or not! (light applause). Alright then Eigi, do you really like Yoko?"

"Yes."

"Noooo! Sorry, wrong answer! (light flashes and people laugh at this). You really don't like Yoko (more laughter and Eigi looks puzzled, but smiles good naturedly). Alright, next question. Eigi, if you're going out for dinner, who decides where you'll eat?"

"We both do."

"Wrong again!! HAHAHAHA! (light flashes again, but off cue, which makes the people laugh). Yoko decides! HAHAHAHA!"

"?"

"Okay Eigi. One last question. What did Yoko say when you asked her to marry you?"

"She said 'Yes.'"

"Wrong agaiiiin! (light goes on) She said, and I quote, … 'No.'"

"Wha …?"

By this time, no one is really listening except for me out of sheer curiosity as to where this was going.

"I'm sorry, but we're all out of time. I hope you enjoyed our little presentation!"

On schedule, everyone burst into applause and smiled while Eigi looked a little confused with a rotating flashing red light on his head.

Next on the agenda, after the little quiz show skit, was the cake cutting. In Japan, as in North America, the wedding cake is not always real. However, every Japanese wedding cake resembles the Tower of Babylon. It's about a metre across at the bottom and is at least two metres high. The table itself is about a metre, so the whole business is about ten feet tall. At this point the guests are invited to take pictures of the 'cutting.' On the signal from the M.C., Eigi and Yoko made their way to the cake. The lights were dimmed and the spotlight once again encircled them. Holding the Samurai-sword-cum-cake-knife together, they stopped midway to pose for photos. As soon as the knife was brought down and touched the cake, another fog machine, under the base of the cake, kicked in. Smoke enveloped the bottom of the lit structure and poured out all over the floor and looked very much like one of the Apollo launches. I turned to the guy next to me.

"Houston, we have a problem."

He didn't laugh.

After the cake had cooled its engines, the M.C. announced that Yoko and Eigi would now leave the room to change into their final we-are-now-leaving outfits. While that happened, the staff of the wedding plaza went around to the tables and distributed the standard wedding thank-you-for-coming gifts to each guest. Everyone received a glossy papered, handled bag consisting of different kinds of foods along with a set of Japanese bowls. If you attend only a few weddings in your lifetime, you'll never want for a bowl again.

By the time the bags were distributed, and mingling guests found their seats, another announcement heralded the couple's last entrance for the evening. For the final time that night, the lights were dimmed, the fog machine over the door came on, and the newlyweds emerged into the spotlight once again. Upon entering the room near the back, they gave their respective parents gifts, lots of bowing ensued, everyone else was thanked via the convenience of a cordless mike, and that was it.

From start to finish, it was over in two hours. Two hours on the button. No loitering. As soon as we left, the staff swarmed the place to set up for the next group and the whole show was put on again. During the peak wedding season, it is not uncommon for one room to be utilized at least three or more times in the run of a day, and to have three or more rooms going at the same time. It's the business to be in.

The last noticeable expense of the day was the transportation. As most weddings take place in either the bride's or groom's hometown, it means transporting your guests to the wedding site. Yoko and Eigi hired two highway buses to take all the guests from where they worked in Matsumoto, to Yokohama (near Tokyo), three hours away.

It was a beautiful bus with a uniformed tour conductor whose only function from what I could tell was to inform us that we were leaving, and then three hours later, to inform us that we were arriving. The only drawback was that Eigi and Yoko neglected to hire a bus with a toilet. A minor inconvenience on the way there, but after hours of continuous race-the-clock beer drinking, the lavatory is just one amenity you can't do without.

It didn't take long for things to start to happen. The bus was caught in the regular weekend Tokyo traffic on the highway and there was no way we could wait. We had no other option but to use a make-shift urinal out of the empty beer cans we had so just greedily emptied. And let me tell you, my friends, that was no easy trick on a moving bus. After the tenuous mission was accomplished, it was a long bus ride to make with two warm beer cans perched on my knees. Any and all bumps in the road were not at all appreciated.

Upon our arrival four hours later, we made a bee-line for the station's washroom to relieve both ourselves and the cans, which in itself was an interesting sight. After all the day's activities, it was finally time to go home, and it was only seven o'clock.

Life

Momma Charis

Ten of my favourite meaningless English phrases found, for some reason, on almost every bicycle chain guard:

"Lettuce Avenue—
How did you Spend Your Vacation"

"Blend—
For Your Lasting Friendship"

"Ralph—
We Enjoyed the Cycling Very Much"

"Lemon Lucifer—
Best Life Cycle Enjoy Time"

"Rivage—
The Record Breaker, Leading the Play, Star of the Game,
Knows Training,
Strength and Discipline. Everyone's Hero"

"Dime—
Become Popular Among People!"

"Ralph—
The Base of Richness is Individuality"

"Hi-Armo—
Have a Good Time on Your Bicycle. You Find the Fantastic Moment."

"Pretty Cattreya—
Bicycle is Fine Sport. For Health and Beauty and Interesting"

"Patio Box—
I can see the Humanity."

Bicycles and The Tofu Man

There are roughly 125 million people in Japan. There are roughly 250 million bicycles in Japan (personal estimate). What do these numbers tell you?

Regardless of how many cars are manufactured and sold in Japan, the bicycle is still perhaps the most common form of transportation. An obvious drawback is that the cyclists live in fear of carbon monoxide poisoning due to millions of cars and lax emissions laws. With the sheer number of people living in the bigger cities, and even the smaller ones for that matter, the bicycle is still the quickest way around town.

Sometimes distance, however, can be a little too much for a bike, so the train becomes the next form of preferred transportation. The Japanese rail system is renowned for its incredible punctuality and endless kilometres of track that will take you anywhere you need to go, usually much faster and more cheaply than going by car. With such extensive use of bicycles and trains, cars become somewhat obsolete and are often relegated to a kind of expensive lawn ornament (if Japanese homes had lawns).

The basic bicycle is referred to as a Momma Chari, loosely translated as 'Mother's Chariot.' They're your basic cast-iron weight bike with a black basket, a skirt-friendly dropped crossbar, wide triangular seat (the kind my mother loves but has never used since 1952), high handlebars, and a carrier over the rear fender. Some of these bad-boys actually come in a five-speed model for the moms who need that extra acceleration when the cross-walk light changes. Others don't have a chain but are belt-driven.

Whoa.

Other features in this line of bikes are the ever present clanking chain guard, and brakes that squeal loudly enough to send dogs within ear-shot into paroxysms.

As implied earlier, many people have two bikes and the reason is simple: one is for riding to the train station from the house, and the other is for riding from the end station to the office or school. As you may have imagined, trying to find your black bike clone from among the other forty million crammed into the station's bike parking area is an exercise in divine inspiration, or mutual theft. This needle-in-a-haystack situation often drives the normal citizen to crime by taking just any ole black bike with a basket.

My mother's solution to this dilemma would be to tie a big plastic red carnation to her bike, much like she does to the aerial of her car, making it easy to locate in any parking lot. Admittedly it works, but I found it highly embarrassing to drive around with when I borrowed the car during my high school years.

That aside, Momma Charis are used by commuters or moms toting kids in bicycle baby-seats. The Post Office uses them during peak seasons for delivering New Year's cards. Some small restaurants in bigger cities will use them for delivering take-out orders to the numerous office buildings that are accessible only through narrow alley-like streets. And in our neighbourhood, we are privileged to be regularly visited by one of the last great practitioners of the full-time working bicycle: The Tofu Man.

The Tofu Man is approximately 243 years old and rides a bicycle of the same vintage and weight in pounds. It has a seemingly solid metal frame with fenders, steel brakes, a seat using the whole hide of a cow, a lamp on the front that appears to use a candle, and tires bigger than most motorcycles. On the back carrier is a steel box roughly 2' by 1.5' by 1.5'. Inside are green plastic containers full of freshly made tofu.

Every Monday and Thursday night he visited the congregation of small apartment complexes where Caroline and I lived. He announced his presence from a distance by blowing a small kazoo-like horn as he meandered through the winding streets. His high-pitched bleat, followed by the yelping of dogs, announced his arrival. Gingerly, the old man would get off his bike, careful not to tip the load, and hoist the bike up onto its kickstand. Then the women would come out of their apartments to buy his rubbery white wares. In just a few minutes his business was done. With a tip of his red baseball cap, he moved his Sherman tank off the kickstand and, trumpeting his approach, crept on to the next clump of dwellings.

One must appreciate that his is no easy feat. It is rumoured that the approximate length of tarmac needed to stop this mass once set in motion is equivalent to that needed to land the space shuttle. Perhaps that's the trick to propelling such a load. Start on an incline, and then immediately apply the brakes in order to stop by the first group of homes some 400 metres away.

Growing up, I would have never eaten tofu. The terror of lima beans was enough. I thought that kind of food was for super-models or people who lived in VW vans and wore tie-dyed T-shirts. However, I started being a lover of the mushed soy beans at roughly the same time that I began shaving my legs.

"Hmm. What's he saying?" you ask. Shaving my legs was part of the rites of passage to being a true competitive cyclist. It has a variety of advantages, one of which being the way it feels when I put on my spandex shorts. But that's something else again. My training program required me to eat lots of protein, and little fat. Thus the Tofu Man entered my life.

It wasn't a quick transition either. The thought of tofu still made me squeamish, but after much coaxing at a restaurant one time, I tried tofu steak. A block of tofu is taken and cut into thick slices, then rolled and dipped in a batter which is then fried with sesame seeds and oil. Add some soy sauce, and there you go. Tofu even the most meat-and-potatoed man could enjoy. After a few tries of that, I was ready to take it straight.

We started buying from the guy about three years ago. Even if we didn't need any, we'd buy anyway to help lighten his load. It's pretty amazing for someone that age out there to be pushing the pedals on that bike through the rain, snow and freezing cold. You'd be hard pressed in any free society to find an individual, besides the Tofu Man, doing such intense physical labour for such little pay. Yes sir, we must pay homage to the Tofu Man now as times they are a changing. You'll rarely see a Tofu Man under 167 years old. Once they shuffle off this mortal coil, it'll be slimy store-bought tofu for the lot of us. There are no whipper-snippers in their nineties waiting to fill their esteemed ranks. Perhaps in the near future, there will be tour groups waiting in the bushes around our apartment with cameras, binoculars, and the latest *Michelin's Tofu Man Watchers Guide* in hand.

"People, quite please! I think we've got one coming now! Shhh!"

Bleeeeeat.

"I can't believe we're going to see one in real life. He looks so old."

The new eco-tourists huddle in the shrubbery and the guide whispers.

"You know, scientists have calculated their ages by ...."

"By counting their rings!"

"Goodness no, we don't do that any more. No, we calculate it by measuring the angle from their shoulders to their knees and subtract a computer generated constant which happens to be three hundred. Thus, by using your protractors on this old gentleman here, we can see the shoulder-to-knee angle is 75 degrees, thereby making him ..."

"Two hundred and twenty five?"

"Excellent."

Our Tofu Man usually made a slow loop of our parking area before heading out to the next stop. Most times, I'd stick my head out the window and say "Tofu please," then scramble to find a suitable container and the correct change. One time, I was a little slow and the Tofu Man made it to our door before I could meet him at his bike.

With one hand he was holding the container of tofu aloft, and with the other he appeared to be fondling the handlebars of my mountain bike with front suspension. I shouted.

"Back off!"

I'm only kidding.

"Nice eh?"I showed him how much travel the suspended front forks got. His eyes widened and he slowly uttered, "Wow."

The Tofu Man is not known for making speeches.

I could see the gears turning over in his head as he silently calculated how much more tofu he could lug around if he had a bike with dual suspension. "Time to modernize. Gotta keep up with the times," he was probably thinking. Personally, I think he was just standing there asleep with his eyes open. Anyway, it was time for business. Other thoughts could wait.

"*Hai.*" (Yes)

He had now turned his attention away from the bike and was looking at me, ready to make the exchange from his tofu dish to mine.

"*Hai.*" I said back as I extended my Tupperware-like container.

"Splop."

The tofu hit the pavement at my feet. The old gent completely missed my bowl and dropped the whole deal on my front porch. I stood with my empty bowl, still extended in front of me, and looked at him for some reaction. He stood there looking at me. After a moment of silence, he mentioned the oft-paid price hoping to jar me into action. After all, he was a busy man.

"That's 230 yen."

"I know. But next time, could you put it in my bowl?" I pointed towards my feet.

"What?"

Slowly his tired head followed my gaze to the pavement directly in front of me.

"Oh crap. Sorry about that," was his reply, crudely translated.

He shuffled off to his bike for another batch and I followed with my awaiting bowl. This time, and from then on, he'd take my wrist with his left, and dump with his right.

I cleaned up the mess and threw the wasted tofu at the eco-tourists lurking in the bushes nearby as my old friend trumpeted his departure from me and his approach to the next clump of houses around the corner.

Big Mac Attack

Most of my communication tragedies were the result of my misunderstanding or misuse of Japanese. In the following, the tables where turned for once in my favour, but the end result was the same.

In my first year in Matsumoto, I started cycling as more than just a means of transportation. One of my students, Ichiro, offered to take me up Utsukushigahara by bike, from whose summit he assured me I would be able to see Mt. Fuji, provided the weather was clear. Naturally.

We arranged to meet at nine o'clock that Sunday next to the 7-11 store near the factory. On that morning, I was all psyched to go with my new mountain bike, helmet, bike shorts, etc. and carried a knapsack with all the essentials (extra water, food, jacket, space blanket ...) When I arrived at the appointed place, there was Ichiro riding what appeared to be a fifteen-year-old ten-speed with drop handle bars, fenders, and carriers over both the front and rear wheels. He was wearing casual slacks with street shoes and had his pant leg tucked into his white sock. He didn't seem to have any food or extra clothes except for the nylon shell jacket he was wearing. In contrast, I was beginning to think that perhaps I was a little over prepared and was reconsidering bringing the Coleman camp stove.

Standing next to Ichiro was another student, Hiro, who had decided to join us. I was a little surprised, as in the first few weeks of classes, he had shown little to no interest in English, let alone socializing with me.

You know how sometimes when you meet a person for the first time and right away you don't like them? For no obvious reason, just like that, you know you're not meant to spend enjoyable time together.

"Nice to meet you"

"You too."

And both of you are thinking, "I don't like this guy. Got shifty eyes."

Maybe he took your parking spot in a past life, but there it is. The grudge has carried over. Hiro is one such person. His apparent laissez-faire attitude towards studying only entrenched this feeling for me. That then is why I have taken great care and pain, to give you as honest and unbiased description of Hiro as possible.

He looks like an alien.

He's a small man with a pasty white body, large head, big round black eyes, and no lips to speak of. There now. I think that was pretty fair.

I'm sure I looked rather conspicuous to him wearing my flashy multicoloured lycra with a body that was not meant to wear it. He was wearing cotton rugby pants and a beige dress shirt with the top two buttons undone and the sleeves rolled up. After all, it was summer.

Hiro's steed was the standard-issue black, one-speed Momma Chari complete with a basket which held his lunch. We made a fine trio. And so the three of us started off.

Ichiro was first, then Hiro and finally me, labouring much harder and being gapped by the other two. Maybe Hiro's lunch was lighter than mine.

And so it went. We followed the river up the valley and into the narrow roads that started to wind up the mountainside. If I could have caught my breath for even a moment and been able to raise my head off the handle bars, I would have noticed that we were making our way through all kinds of vineyards in one of the best wine-producing areas of Japan. The sun was glorious and warm and the sky a cobalt blue. The vines were thick and made a heavy canopy over the steel frames underneath. The mountains undisturbed by time, welcomed us to climb to the peak. It was truly a glorious day.

Personally, I was ready to up-chuck.

My pride wouldn't let me fall off the back for long and I made way up to Ichiro, utilizing all of my twenty-one gears to Hiro's one. On the really steep sections, Hiro got off and pushed while I dropped down into my easiest gear and spun like a mad man, only to have to dismount ten metres later, from oxygen deprivation. It was like a terrible dream where your legs turn to jelly. I could see, between gasps, Hiro advancing towards me pushing his bike. I wanted desperately to remain ahead of him and his one-speed bike. But my legs ignored the pleas from my brain to move. His expressionless cold black eyes never even looked for a moment in my direction. Yet, I could feel them mocking me and my twenty-one gears and flashy clothes, as they quietly passed and went effortlessly around the next corner.

At that moment, I wished bad things upon him.

By the time we had our second scheduled break, I had inhaled every morsel I brought. Hiro's lunch was untouched. I've heard aliens don't eat. Trying to make friendly conversation on an otherwise totally mute trip, I innocently announced, "Man, I could really go for a Big Mac right now."

To which Hiro almost shouted at me, "No! No Big Mac here!" eyes a-blinking.

I was surprised to say the least. First that Hiro would voice such a strong objection to my craving, and second, thinking his eyelids were the biggest ones I had ever seen. I could almost hear them close when he blinked.

"What do you mean, 'No Big Mac here?' I know there are no Big Macs here, but I'm saying I want a Big Mac."

He repeated, "No Big Mac here! Nobody has Big Mac here. You no have Big Mac here too."

By this time, my hunger and exhaustion coupled with his inexplicable and smug ability to outpace me as we rode forged a stubborness in me. Going farther than I should, I said rather nonchalantly, "Ya know Hiro (if that's your real name), I could have a Big Mac right here if I wanted to. In fact, I can have a Big Mac anywhere I please. I could have one in my classroom in fact, and there's not a thing you could do about it."

He gave me a look of contempt usually reserved for those people who pick their nose and then eat it (not that I've ever done that), grabbed his bike and continued up the mountain leaving a silent Ichiro and me behind.

We continued on in silence for a while, and with each minute I felt more and more guilty for being so boorish on the Big Mac issue. I'm sure he had his reasons, and after all, I was the guest on this adventure. Finally, Ichiro who had been privy to the whole encounter spoke up for what I believe was the first time this trip.

"Erik san, I think when you say Big Mac, Hiro thinks you mean going to toilet sitting down. Make number two."

Who teaches these guys?

"Oh… I see."

What else could I say? The damage was done. He said no more and we carried on as I replayed the dialogue with Hiro in my mind, replacing Big Mac with Number Two.

From that point on in Hiro's eyes, I was an unclean, plundering, unsophisticated, barbarian who had Big Macs everywhere and anywhere I pleased.

As it turned out, I never really saw Hiro around much after that day. Perhaps he was called back to the Mother ship. Regardless, I have a sneaking suspicion that he started spreading rumours around the factory about my propensity of having Big Macs at random. I also think that in the early days of my living here, these rumours prevented a lot of dinner invitations from being offered. I've since learned, when I'm hungry, to express a craving for Japanese food only. If you want to avoid the Big Mac hitting the fan, you'll do the same.

Peter Pan Complex

This particular miscommunication is special to me. That's because for once, it involves Caroline, and not myself. You must understand. Caroline, as wonderful and kind as she is, seems to derive great pleasure in pointing out the fact that her Japanese language ability is far superior to mine, which isn't saying much, as most sea-lions have a greater language ability than I do.

In our fair city, there is a bakery that we frequent. Unlike most commercial breads that reek of formaldehyde, the bread at Komatsu's Bakery is fresh each morning. Regular customers can have standing orders for their particular favourites. Caroline wanted to place an order for pita bread. Even though she had never seen pita in the shop, she felt they could make it for her. How hard could it be? She decided to get a weekly standing order.

"I'd like to place a standing order starting next week please."

"Certainly. What would you like?"

"I'd like six pitas please."

"Six … what?"

"Six pitas for next week."

The baker looked at her and simply shrugged his shoulders that he didn't understand. Thinking it was a straightforward request, Caroline tried again. The next effort made things just that much more difficult, as the word used for "bread" in Japanese is the same as in French: "*pan*." Therein lies the rub.

"I ... would ... like ... six ... pita ... *pans* ... please."

"You want six Peter Pans for next week?"

"Yes, yes, that's right! Six pita *pans*."

"Peter Pans?"

After this he pretended to fly around the shop like the green-leotard-clad star of Never Never Land. It was Caroline's turn to stare as bemused customers looked on.

"What the hell is he doing?"

The baker kept doing laps back and forth behind his counter with his arms stretched out in front of him saying, "Peter Pan, Peter Pan," and looking at Caroline for confirmation.

Click.

"Ohhhh!" Caroline said, and laughed. The baker stopped flying and the rest of the customers went about their business as Caroline finally drew him a picture of what she wanted.

Every time we go in there now, the baker gives us a little smile and puts his arms out in front of him and says 'Peter Pan' while swaying back and forth. Yes, yes. Ha, Ha.

Kanji and Plato

There is definitely a similarity between the constellations and *kanji*. What I mean is that the pictorial representation in the strokes of the *kanji*, or the Chinese characters, which are used in the written form of Japanese, are about as easy to see as it is to see the detailed outline of Orion in a cluster of three or four vague stars.

Kanji characters are stylized pictures of the word they represent. Many beginner texts use the words 'mountain' (*yama*) or 'river' (*kawa*) to demonstrate. It seems simple at first and you're smiling to yourself at how clever you are. Then you turn to page two and have all your dreams of being the great communicator in Japanese dashed against the jagged rocks of reality. But let's not get ahead of ourselves. Let's look at page one first.

This is the *kanji* character for '*yama*' (mountain). You can see a mountain there.

And here's the character for *'kawa'* (river). Flowing water. That looks reasonable.

And now, here are the characters for *'ichi, ni, san'* (one, two, three) Pretty simple so far.

No complaints. Ha! Given what one, two and three look like, what do you think 'four' is? Turn to page two of the Japanese text and think again.

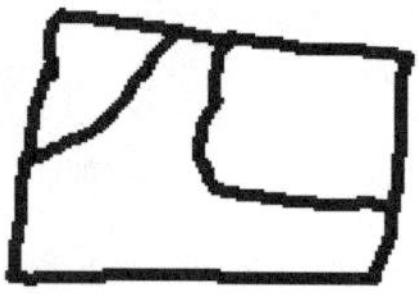

It gets worse. Thankfully Arabic numbers are used on a daily basis, otherwise Japanese calculators would require their own Rosetta stones.

For another example, take a look at this one. It means person.

Yet the symbol for 'person' is not consistent when used with another *kanji* character in order to form a different word. Take this *kanji* character.

It means 'holiday.' Can you see it? Obviously the strokes represent a 'man' who is relaxing under a tree. Hence, 'holiday' or 'a day off work.' What? You don't see it? Look again.

Perhaps you're better at picking up languages than I am, but I think these connections are a bit of a stretch of the imagination. Try this one.

It means 'colour.' The representation of the word is done by depicting a man and a woman, procreating in a non-missionary position. I guess that's

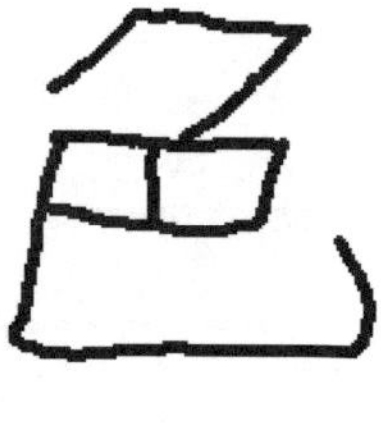

the only way it was done given the fact that there probably were no missionaries in China at that time. At least, that's the way it was explained to me. The word then for 'sexy,' pronounced '*iipoi'* literally means, 'colourful.' It's bad enough trying to see what the image is, let alone trying to guess what kind of seemingly random connection it has to an actual word.

From my own observations, I have drawn the conclusion that the stylization of pictures to form *kanji* makes about as much sense as being able to pick out a picture from the constellations using just a few pin pricks of light in the night sky. I mean, how can you get an epic battle taking place between a lion and a man with a drawn sword from this?

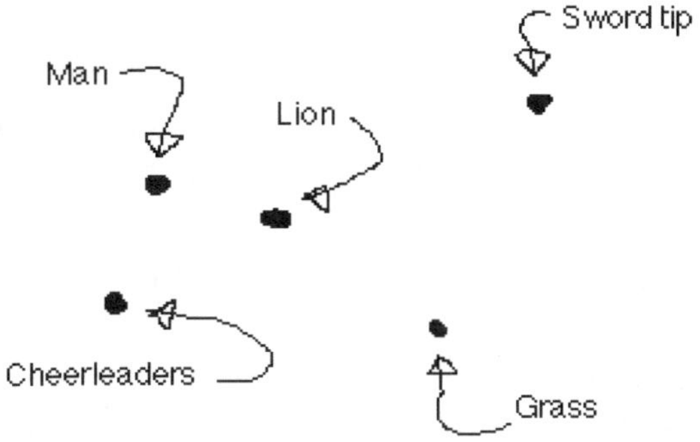

It just doesn't wash. And what great sage decided all of this stuff anyway? Was it Plato? I can imagine Plato, looking up at the stars, everything just ticketyboo until some wise guy has to ask, 'What do those stars represent, O great teacher?'

Now he's on the spot. His students are all looking up to him for some kind of answer. Their parents had to put up a lot of money to send them to the Academy so he had to come up with an answer or he could kiss next term's tuition money goodbye.

"Well … uhm … if you connect the stars like dots on a page, they will form a picture of great significance."

"What picture?"

"Uhm, okay. See that star over there. The one that's really bright and is at the tip of that thing that looks like a big spoon? That's the tip of ... of Orion's Sword! Now over there, that brightish star is the base of Orion's heel. Finally, umm, that star a little above is the end of a lion's tail which, as you can plainly see, Orion is doing battle with. It's all right there. Okay then ... who's up for some Platonic Wrestling, eh?"

Come on. How can those three stars depict such a picture? On the other hand, who was going to argue with Plato? After all, he was the founder of the Academy, and he ought to know, right?

Time and time again, civilization has betrayed itself by not questioning the wisdom of some goofy notion their exhalted leader had. Look at Troy. They had it pretty good until Zeus wanted Paris to decide which of the goddesses was most beautiful. Having chosen Aphrodite, he was granted the most beautiful woman in the world, Helen. Sounds pretty good, until you consider that Helen was already married. To the king of Greece no less. What business did Aphrodite have promising Helen to Paris as a way of saying 'thanks for your vote' in the first place?

It would seem a tad unrealistic that Paris would think the king of Greece would let it slide and simply say, "Oh, Paris came and got my wife while I was away and Aphrodite said it was okay. Well then, no problem. She always ate with her mouth open anyway. 'Smack, smack, smack.' I hated that. So ... what's on at the amphitheater tonight?"

No sir. It didn't happen that way. Because Paris figured the most beautiful woman in the world was his, he caused his city and empire to be destroyed. Duh! And for what? For Helen? She chews with her mouth open for Heaven's sake.

All of these examples bring us to the final and perhaps ultimate lack-of-questioning-blunder in the last few millennia — *kanji*.

It originally came from China to Japan, a very long time ago, and was probably devised by someone who no one would question. My guess is the person responsible for this linestroke representation hullabaloo was Confucius. He seemed the type. I mean, look at the guy. Always shuffling around in a housecoat and talking in circles. Could you imagine how annoying that'd be? You'd never get a straight answer.

"Would you like some tea?"

"Tea is but an extension of our eternal soul."

"... Is that a *yes*?"

I can imagine that after having taught his first *kanji* lesson, Confucius asked his students: "Any questions ... ?"

And nobody said anything. If even one of them had the guts to say, "Hey. I don't think that looks like a man relaxing under a tree at all. In fact, I don't think ANYBODY thinks that looks like a man under a tree!" then maybe the world would be a much different place. At least for me.

You see, no one questioned Paris' move. No one questioned Plato (or whoever) about what pictorial the stars represented. And no one questioned what the strokes of the *kanji* represented. If someone questioned what the *kanji* represented and demanded a more realistic portrayal of the word, then maybe I'd be able to read a Japanese newspaper this very day. Granted, the destruction of Troy is a little more weighty than my inability to read the paper.

To make it that much harder, written Japanese encompasses three different styles of writing. First, there's *kanji*, (Chinese characters), then *hiragana* (a 52-character phonetic style like the alphabet which allows the reader to sound out any word) and finally, *katakana* (like *hiragana*, but with different characters used solely for foreign words that don't have a *kanji* equivalent).

Combining these three together makes Japanese one of the hardest, if not the hardest, written language in the world. A friend told me that. He said his university professor said it. And if it came from a professor, then who am I to question it?

I feel much better.

Julianna's Disco and The Law (Part One)

As I've said, I work for a fairly large company with about eight factories, two of which have full-time English teachers. I'm one, and Don, the person I replaced in Matsumoto, works three hours east by train in the Tokyo factory.

Not so long ago, it was arranged for me to take a business trip to swap ideas and teaching material with Don in Tokyo. I was to go Sunday and come back Monday night. Around that time on the news, there had been reports of this notorious Disco, Julianna's. As I didn't get out much, I thought it'd be a hoot to go. The reason it's famous/infamous is that all, or almost all the women patrons wear 'Body Con' dresses. This is a Japanese/English term referring to outfits that seem to be painted on with a spandex based material and whose bottom hem must not go any lower than five centimetres below where the legs meet at the top. Hence, girls wearing such revealing outfits, must be very *conscious* of their *bodies*. Get it?

In addition to that, the girls wear three- to four-inch spike pumps, get up on three-tier, pyramid-shaped stages in the corner of the dance floor and gyrate to endless, wordless, Techno-Eurobeat (music?) played at ear-bleeding volumes. I wanted to go to say I went, and Don being the ever accommodating host, agreed to go. I didn't exactly have to twist his arm.

It being a Sunday night, we didn't anticipate a very large crowd, but as it turned out, Sunday night was Ladies' Night. Women got in free while the rest of us paid the sixty dollars U.S. cover charge. As we approached the building we noticed everybody's attire looked quite normal. Nothing out of the ordinary. Was all the hoopla just an urban myth?

Inside the front door there was a co-ed locker room to store your jacket, etc. I was stuffing our coats into a tiny locker, and couldn't help but notice the girls next to us, and all around us for that matter. They were all taking off their pants and tops to reveal the spandexed Body Con dresses of legend and lore, which they had kept hidden under their normal street clothes, away from disapproving parents' eyes. The sneakers were replaced by stiletto heels kept in the shoulder bag. A little tug here and there, a lot of bright pink lipstick applied and away they went into the wall of music.

The metamorphosis I witnessed in the locker room was conservative compared to those already inside. The general rule of thumb was 'the more risqué, the better.' The traditional Julianna's undergarment was the 'T-back.' Named after its shape, of course. While dancing on these little stages, the girls would get caught up in the frenzied music and lights, and start lifting their skirts higher and higher. There is not a lot of leeway here, and soon the bottoms of their dresses would be hiked up around their hips, exposing their T-back undies. Now, this is not a men's club, and the girls are not being paid; it's just the fashion. It's not a tiny club either. It easily holds six hundred plus.

This form of dancing soon found itself on the news, prompting other young girls in other discos around the country to do the same thing. Not to be outdone by their country cousins, the regulars at Julianna's decided it was time for a bolder move. Girls started taking off their tops, and some weren't bothering with the T-backs at all. More conservative girls were wearing 'O' backs, which were dresses that had a big circle cut out over their behind, letting the 'cheeks' poke out. I was definitely not in Kansas anymore. I am told they don't do it as a sexual come-on but more of a form of rebellion against a strict and orderly society. Granted, the disrobing dance is not a regular event, but rather, tends to happen at random. We were not to see this first hand that night, but it was on the news ....

After I got over the initial shock of what people were wearing, I noticed a definite social hierarchy. The little stages on the corners are called *todachidai* and they are coveted territory. One girl dominates the top level of the pyramid, while three girls are on the next and three again on the last. Pity the girl who unwittingly grabs the top spot if she doesn't belong there. The girls on the lower level aspire to one day gyrate on the top. Getting and staying on the top spot seemed to be determined by how long you can dance on a one foot square space without going to the bathroom.

I watched as one of the girls on the top spot, who had been dancing quite confidently all evening, got down for a much needed 'pee' break. As soon as she was out of sight, a girl from a lower level made a grab for the pinnacle to show her stuff. She didn't last long. When the first girl returned, the girl now on top was visibly nervous as she got caught where she didn't belong. To make things worse, she couldn't get down quickly enough because someone else had grabbed her spot on the lower level. Those ones are first come, first dance. The previous prima donna was outraged and began to berate the other girl until she managed to slink off the pyramid with her head down and lose herself in the throbbing crowd. The girls on the lower level made room for Numero Uno and she took her place again on top with a defiant flip of her hair and a rotation of her hips. The Law of the Jungle.

Julianna's Disco (Part Two): Getting Home

Alas, the magical night of enchantment came unceremoniously to an end. Unfortunately, closing time did not coincide with the last train to Hachioji, where Don's apartment was, some twenty kilometres away.

It was February and cold. The next train wasn't until five a.m. It was now one-thirty a.m. and I didn't want to wait and Don didn't want to walk. While shuffling around in circles near the station trying to keep warm, we noticed a small patch of grass that had two trashed Momma Charis covered in grass. They were old and rusty, definitely abandoned. One had a flat tire (I gave that one to Don), and the other's handle bars were bent. So off we went to cycle the twenty kilometres to Hachioji.

The clanking of our chains against the twisted chain guards was amplified between the silent towering concrete buildings as we wove our way down the deserted downtown streets. Well … we thought they were deserted.

Fifteen minutes into our little journey, we were ambushed. Before we knew it, policeman swarmed upon us, riding white Momma Charis with the word 'POLICE' stenciled down the sloping cross bar.

"You've got to be joking," I thought.

But they weren't. Two were beside me and three were

beside Don. They wanted us to pull over. I had heard of the police occasionally harassing foreigners but to this date I had never had any trouble. I kept pedaling away and smiling as if to say, "Nice night for a ride, isn't it Constable!" They started to get a little antsy, squeezed in a bit and signaled for us to follow them. Given their general physical condition, i.e., had one too many doughnuts over the years, I thought just for a moment that we should try to out-run them. Glancing at my wobbling handlebars and Don's flat tire and pleading face not to, I decided to go peacefully. I started to smile as I pictured what our little pedal-cade must have looked like from a pedestrian's perspective.

We were taken to a little community police station called, appropriately, a Police Box. Once inside we were told to empty our pockets. The police officer behind the counter picked up the book of matches I had taken from the disco. He smiled.

"Julianna's. Good?"

"Good." I replied in English. Perhaps this wasn't going to go so badly after all. Maybe they'd even give us a lift to Don's place. Then suddenly the tone changed when another policeman came in.

"Whose bicycles are those?" he demanded in Japanese.

"We don't know," Don said, acting as our spokesperson. "We found them in the garbage."

"You stole them, didn't you!" His voice was rising a little bit too much for my comfort, but somehow I don't think my comfort was what they had in mind.

"No, no, we didn't steal them. They were in the garbage and we borrowed them to get back to my apartment." Mistake.

"Where's that?"

"Hachioji," Don answered.

"You were going to bicycle all the way to Hachioji on those bikes?" He asked incredulously.

"That's right. We missed the last train, so we thought we'd use those bikes from the garbage to get home."

Our friend just snorted to that and moved into a huddle with his comrades, discussing their next move with this gang of international bike rustlers. Finally the huddle broke and the friendlier cop came over. "Come with us."

Yahoo. A ride home.

Don and I climbed into the back of one of the cruisers and with a police car in front of ours, and another in back, we took off with the red lights flashing. We weren't going home just yet. We were going downtown.

Talk about police intimidation. We arrived at the main station around 2:30 a.m. in a three-car motorcade. The occupants of the fore and aft cars hopped out and surrounded ours. As we stepped out, we were quickly ushered up the steps. There were two of us, and nine of them. Doughnuts weren't on their minds tonight. They had apprehended some gen-u-ine international antique crappy bike criminals.

As we entered the station, all noise ceased. Heads swiveled. Everyone wanted to catch a glimpse of the evening's big shakedown. I wanted to yell above my escort's heads a la James Cagney.

"It wasn't me shee! I was framed I tell ya! Framed!"

They took us upstairs. We were seated in the squad room filled with curious cops writing reports, when the same line of questioning began and to which we responded with the same answers.

"We've told you. We missed the last train and were walking home to ..."

"To Hachioji?" one wanted to clarify.

"Yes. To Hachioji. Then we saw these bikes in the grass and as they were obviously garbage, we thought we'd ... "

"Bike to Hachioji," another finished with a touch of sarcasm.

"Yes. That's right. To Hachioji," I finished and for the first time that evening realized that the idea of cycling all that way on those beat-up bikes now seemed a little far-fetched even to me.

The interrogators huddled again, and there was a lot of murmuring and looking over of shoulders. Don, the Japanese veteran, seemed nervous, which made me nervous. Perhaps he knew the penalty for illegal use of abandoned broken down bicycles was a little more severe than I first thought. Perhaps Don had been mixed up with an abandoned bicycle theft before? Then I starting thinking how comforting it was to know that in a city this size, some sixteen million people, in this part of town, at this time of night, the biggest action going down was us. Public safety doesn't get much safer than that. This revelation was fine for the common Joe San all snug in his bed, knowing that his long forgotten and discarded bike in the weeds was safe while he slept. But for us, it meant some rookie would be trying to make a name for himself with this case. You gotta work with what you get. If you get lemons, make lemonade. If you get would-be bike rustlers, go for the death penalty.

After an inordinate amount of time, discussion, and over-the-shoulder stern expressions, the huddle broke. A decision had been made. If asked, I would say no to the blindfold and yes to the cigarette. Be a man. Instead, two forms were taken from a desk and laid in front of us with a bit of theatrics. A pause for effect, then, in a quiet and slow tone it was explained. If we co-operated and signed these papers we would be allowed to go. In effect we would be signing a confession. The wording said that we were greatly sorry and grieved by our misdeeds and humbly apologized for any wrongdoings. I believed one section mentioned we were scurvy dogs. If we signed, this confession would stay in the confines of this particular office (only to be shown around at retirement parties) and our company need not be informed. That was their ace-in-the hole, as it is with any offence. Telling your wife, family, or friends is a negligible threat compared to the threat of telling your company.

The social hierarchy of the company can dictate an employees' life outside the company as well as inside. Most common criminals think: "You can beat me, whip me, cover me in honey and feed me to the ants, but for the love of Buddha, don't tell my commmmpaaaannnnnnyyy!! (sob, whimper)"

If you consider that many Japanese people have their status of employment determined from the time they're in elementary school, (going to the right kind of school starts in kindergarten), and that their current lifestyle status is defined by their job, they're not going to want to disturb that. There is nothing much worse than being kicked out of your company. Being outside the corporate loop, you're outside of society, and that is like falling into an abyss from which you can never return. That analogy may seem a bit severe for us, but not for them.

You may also be thinking, "What if the guy's unemployed?" Fear not. A lot of criminals end up turning themselves in. The newspaper ran an account of a man in his forties who had robbed a bank in the middle of the morning, making a clean getaway. By mid-afternoon, the man's wife (soon-to-be 'ex-wife' I'm sure) came back to the bank to return the money her husband had stolen and apologized on her husband's behalf. Can you imagine? She returned the money and apologized. No wonder the police can boast of a 90 % success rate. I suppose the ones they didn't get tried to turn themselves in after working hours. Maybe they should leave a recorded message on their telephone answering machine saying:

Thank you for calling the Metropolitan Police station. All our operators are busy at the moment. Please leave a message after the beep. If you have an emergency and need to talk to someone in person press 'one' now. If you'd like to turn yourself in for stealing an umbrella or bicycle, press 'two.' Press 'three' for grand larceny, 'four' for fraud, and 'five' for homicide. If you are unable to come to the station, please hold the line and an officer service representative will be with you in a moment to make arrangements to have you picked up. Also, make sure you bring all crime-related evidence with you to ensure a speedy sentencing. Thank you. It will be a pleasure arresting you!

Of course there are bound to be a few mavericks who don't play by the rules, or who don't have loved ones to turn them in. I guess they also make up part of the ten percent that got away.

So anyway, here we are back at the police station with the confession in front of us, ready to sign.

The clock ticked.

The police stared.

Don wept.

Okay, he didn't weep, but it sounded good. I quickly tried to assess the situation. If I didn't sign, what could they do? I mean, I know that no one was claiming the bike. I knew it was garbage and I knew they knew it too. Could they deport me for not signing? I doubt it. Could they detain me until I did? Hardly likely. If they called my company, would I be reprimanded in any way? I doubted that too. If the company was called, would they renew my yearly cushy-contract? Probably not. I picked up the pen and signed without giving it another thought.

I couldn't believe it. They got me with the ole, 'We're-gonna-call-your-company' scam. I felt so cheap. Not only did I have to sign, but I had to have my fingerprint taken, just in case some bikes turn up missing. They'll probably be dusting around the crime scene hoping to nab me again. Then the mayor and Police Chief could make a statement to the press about busting another bike cartel. No doubt the article would be accompanied by a picture of the Mayor and the Chief posing with a shovel full of earth, pretending to cover up the bicycles.

Bitter? Perhaps. I was cold and wanted to go home. We were allowed to go and ended up walking to the next local train station where we waited in silence for the first train at five a.m.

The moral of the story? If you're a married man at a bar of ill repute without your wife, trouble will find you one way or another.

Golfing

I am not a golfer. If you watched me play, you'd agree. Yet in Japan there are over twelve million regular golfers (ten percent of the entire population) utilizing a vast 640 golf clubs around the country twenty-four hours a day (true). Some courses are lit for night use with tee-off times at three a.m. No thanks. Yet there are people willing do it, each paying a mind-boggling minimum of $200 U.S. on a public course. I believe that private courses will even accept deeds to downtown Tokyo real-estate or luxury yachts in lieu of green fees.

The little golfing I have done involved carrying my own clubs, washing my own balls, and of course, doing my own cursing. For a mere two hundred dollars a pop, all of this can be done for you.

In Japan, caddies are usually women under five feet tall. Maybe that's some kind of job requisite. Perhaps they use a five-foot-high door frame for interviews. Those who make it under without stooping are put on the Short List. Ha!

Their uniforms are similar to what women wear in the fields when planting or harvesting rice — a bonnet tied under the chin with a wide brim that encircles the face, very much like Little Bo Peep. The blouse is made from heavy, loose cotton and is held in place by a canvas bib which covers the front and back of the caddie. It is all one colour with no markings or designs. Pants are normal workman pants tucked into rubber rain boots. On the hands they quite often wear what looks like yellow rubber dish-washing gloves. Even close up, you'd be very hard pressed to distinguish your caddie, from your partner's.

A friend of mine, Alistair, took the plunge and spent the two hundred dollars to experience golf in Japan. At one point he was standing next to the golf bags, which were on some kind of cart, when all of a sudden they started moving. Startled, he ran after them and grabbed on to the handle to stop them from rolling down the hill. The response to his heroics was stifled giggles from the caddies as they turned off the power switch and stopped the cart remotely.

There is an elaborate underground magnetic system which allows the electric carts to follow the tracks around the outside of the fairways. The miniature caddies follow behind working the remote control, stop along the edge of the fairway closest to your ball, remove the appropriate club, procede onto the course and wait for you. Before you get there, they have picked up your ball, polished it off with a rag, and placed it back down, ready to go. They don't do this every couple of holes, but after every shot.

For those who feel golfing is a sport which expends too much energy, fear not. Some courses even have moving sidewalks, or outdoor escalators for the elevated sections of the fairway.

After finishing the front nine, my friend said that they had to take a break. 'Had to' was the key phrase, as they were not allowed to continue to the back nine unless they had a receipt from the sub-clubhouse that they had purchased something. The sub-clubhouse, as you may have guessed, was at the far end of the course. Your choice at that point was to either buy something and golf your way back, or take a stand and not buy something. This action would end your game, forcing you to walk all the way back to the main clubhouse, in which case I'm sure your escalator privileges would be revoked.

Most people save the real full-fledged golf experience until they've paid off their mortgage or won the lottery. Before that time, the average golfing Joe must be content with the Driving Range.

The word 'range' is used rather loosely. In cities there is not much range to speak of. The golf practice areas are usually two- or three-tier covered platforms that allow a large number of people to drive innocent golf balls into an encompassing hanging green net. Round white markers with the numbers of potential metres you've hit hang like bull's eyes off the back curtain. Depending on the space restrictions, this back net may be fifty metres, or only twenty metres away. This allows any person with a good chip shot to believe they are hitting over 250 metres with their sand wedge.

You'll notice too that even at the driving range, everyone is wearing the proper gear. As with any single activity in Japan, everyone has the best of the best. Beginners or experts have the latest and newest. At the driving range, no one is wearing jeans or cut off shorts. Men wear oddly coloured pants (mostly plaid) and women wear golfing shorts that are loose and come down to the knees. Golfing gloves are a must, as well as shoes. No Pro Ked sneakers in this bunch. Loose fitting golf shirts with sleeveless sweater vests and optional visors or hats complete the ensemble. You may not be able to swing a club to save your life, but you'll look like you can, and with most things in life, that's the key.

Heating the House with Soy Milk

A few years ago, Caroline and I bought a used car. Quite a bargain really. A 1990 Toyota Vista. Two-litre engine, power everything, virtually new interior and only 60,000 kilometres, all for about eight hundred dollars. I normally don't drive the car around town much, as I feel it's faster to go most everywhere by bike, and besides, to fill your gas tank is roughly the same price as you paid for the car in the first place. Anyway, it was a new car for us, and I wanted to take it for a spin. As we needed more kerosene for the space heaters we used in our apartment, I volunteered to take our two, five-gallon plastic storage containers to the gas station to get them filled.

For some unknown reason, the Japanese do not use central heating, nor do they use any kind of real insulation. So the temperature inside is roughly the same outside, plus or minus a few degrees. Instead, they have very high-tech, programmable, kerosene space heaters. Every winter morning sees a quick dash from the warmth of the futon to the shower before the heaters make things livable.

As it worked out, my wanting to take the new car coincided with our needing heating fuel and so away I went.

It was a Sunday night with not much action on the main drag. I pulled into the gas stand with the usual loud amount of yelling and greetings that goes on. Once I had stopped the car, the young uniformed attendant appeared at my door. I nonchalantly hit the power-window button as if to say, "Hey! Look at me hitting the power window button. Dig me." With the window having whirred down into place, I indicated with a casual nod of my head that I wanted him to fill up the five-gallon containers in the trunk with kerosene (*touyu* in Japanese). But what I said was '*tonyu.*' Very similar in sound, but quite different in meaning. The former being a combustible hydro-carbon, the other, soy milk.

The young man looked a little puzzled.

"*Tonyu?*"

"That's right. Please fill up the tanks in the trunk with *tonyu.*"

This brought more frowns and sucking of the teeth, as people do when confronted with a vexing dilemma over here.

"Ahhh. I'm sorry, but we don't have any *tonyu* here."

Now either, I thought, this guy was playing stupid or he was yanking my chain because I was looking right at the *tonyu* pump as we spoke. I became a little sarcastic.

"This is a gas station, is it not?"

"That's right," he answered patiently.

"And you're trying to tell me that you don't sell any *tonyu* here?" I continued in the same tone.

"That's right. We don't sell *tonyu*"

"Well then …" I was on a roll and pointed at the *tonyu* pump with great theatrics. "… if you don't sell any *tonyu*, then what do you call that?"

"That's *touyu*," he answered a little smuggly, though justified.

Nowhere to run and nowhere to hide. "Oh … right. Okay then. I'll take some of that, please (ahem)."

I looked straight ahead and left the windows down as I was feeling a little hot, and anxiously tapping my foot to have the whole process over with. I should have learned a long time ago, if I think someone's making a mistake, that someone is more than likely me. Regardless, Caroline is now in charge of filling the tanks, and buying the soy milk.

Bird Business

One of the things that makes life just that much more interesting living in a different culture is the inevitable, complete and total breakdown in communication between the visitor and host culture. Naturally this is not a good thing when you dial the emergency number to tell them there's been an auto accident outside and to send help, but in fact tell them that the pizza outside has been left under the elephant.

Any miscommunication with civic authorities is also a bad thing, particularly if you're trying to explain the reason behind dumping the contents of a 20-kg brown paper bag into a field late at night, using the headlights of your car to light the way. Dressing like a bum doesn't help either.

One spring Caroline went to city hall and placed our name in a lottery to use one of the city-owned garden plots near our house. The lucky winners, of which there are many, are allotted their own patch of land to till and plant. This is a good thing. Personally, I was against our acquiring one from the beginning because I knew that all roads to weed-infested gardens were paved with good intentions. Upon discovering we were among the lucky winners, I made it quite clear to Caroline that I had no intention whatsoever of having anything to do with a garden at this point in my life. But wanting to be the ever supportive husband, I did offer to eat anything she could grow from it. Hey, I was busy and had no time to devote to anything else.

"Fine. I'll do it myself," she said.

On one of the hottest days of the year, Caroline and her friend Lisa set out to clear the field. It was about 34° C, yet there they were, on their hands and knees, yanking out all the bramble and weeds. After an entire day of drudgery, the little 5 X 5-metre plot was cleared and the rich soil was ready. And that's how it sat for the next two months.

You see, my wife and I suffer from the same problem. We're 'self-starters,' but we're just not 'self-finishers.' For example: Have you ever found yourself on a country road that just ends in the middle of nowhere? I am the kind of guy who would build such a road. In a small corner of Japan, thanks to us, there is a monument to just that kind of thinking. Anyway, at the beginning of May, Caroline flew home for a few months to prepare for our wedding on the East Coast of Canada (it's never too late to send a gift). The task of fertilizing the garden was begrudgingly accepted by moi.

Jason, another teacher in town, happened to live next to a guy who raised pigeons. I don't think these people realize that pigeons don't need to be raised. All they have to do is go to any city park and scoop up all they want into a burlap bag for free. Nonetheless, Jason's neighbour did raise them and in the process would gather all his pigeon's poop into 20-kg paper bags. Our friend asked on our behalf, if he could get a few to help fertilize our garden. The neighbour kindly offered us two bags of his very finest. Jason's work schedule was opposite to mine, so I asked him to leave it outside his apartment where I would pick it up sometime over the next few days.

Two weeks passed and he was now understandably getting a little anxious to see the stuff go. While Caroline was away, I was teaching some of her classes at night while conducting my own during the day. On top of that I was still trying to get a few hours of training in for an upcoming mountain bike race. Regardless, and out of consideration for Jason, I absolutely could not let another day go by before I picked up the 'shit-ment.'

After I got back from a late training session that night, I threw on some old clothes, and headed over to Jason's. I didn't have time to shower, and still had some mud splashed on my face from the bike ride up the rain-soaked mountain. There was nobody home when I got there, so I grabbed the bags and loaded them one at a time into the trunk of my car. Fortunately, the garden site is midway between my house and his, right near the centre of town. It's an out-of-place-looking field surrounded by a bunch of concrete office buildings and contrasting century-old homes.

I soon arrived and sat in a parking lot next to the field. I sat there for the longest time trying to decide just where in the heck our plot was. I had only seen it once when I came to see if Caroline really was digging it up on that hot day, or if she was just sitting there reading a book under a beach umbrella. That was then, this was now.

I remembered seeing on the far left corner of our plot, an old green plastic watering can that someone had left behind. I figured with the highbeams of the car, I'd probably have enough light to find it. I did.

Our little patch wasn't an easy thing to get to in the dark. Each little garden was surrounded by its own mini-moat. The shadows cast by the car's lights over the field played tricks with my depth perception. What in the day was a scant crossing, appeared to be a raging river at night, waiting to pull me into the black abyss, beyond the highbeam's reach. I was looking very much like a stork after one too many wild berries, as I lifted my legs much higher and stepped farther than needed, as I cautiously crossed the irrigation trenches.

After having located our cleared plot, which by this time had a thick stubble of weeds, I weaved my way back to the car and popped the trunk. Grabbing the first bag, I hoisted it onto my shoulder and retraced my steps. At the edge of our garden I dropped the bag on the ground and peered into the shadows to find the best place to unload the contents. It was now after midnight and I was in no mood for fertilizing a garden which I said I would have nothing to do with in the first place. So I emptied the bag at my feet. It was not a callous thing to do, as I promised myself I would come back at a more appropriate time to spread it all around. For now, just one more trip to my car, then back home to a shower and bed. Yet, while all this rationalization was running through my mind, Joe Citizen in a house nearby was having a hushed conversation with the local police station.

"Matsumoto Police. How may we humbly help you?"

"Come quick! There's a foreigner in my garden!"

"A what?"

"There's a foreigner in my garden!"

At this point he was probably thinking that this was some kind of adolescent prank.

"Have you tried a different kind of weed killer?"

Big laughs from his colleague.

"Come on, I'm serious. He was looking for something. Something in the field across from my house. He seemed confused. Like he couldn't remember where he buried something. I couldn't make out where he went, but he looked drunk by the way he was walking."

"Does he have anything? Is he carrying anything?"

"No. I … I … don't think so. Wait. He's back and opened his car and released the trunk. He's lifting out a … a very large brown bag and carrying it into the field. Oh my word! Do you think it's a body?"

"Don't move! Tell us your address and we'll be right there!" He scribbles on his note pad and shouts to his partner. "Come on Masa! We've got a live one tonight!"

"Shouldn't we get some back-up for this?"

"Not a chance. This is going to get us out of the sticks and put us Downtown. Let's go!"

And they did.

I met them as I was fumbling in the trunk for the second bag. Just as I was about to sling the sack over my shoulder, I heard them.

"YOU THERE! What are you doing?"

Startled, I dropped the bag back into the trunk which caused a cloud of pigeon-poop dust to billow up. I turned to face what seemed like a one-million-candle-power flashlight/deathray. I could see the figure of a uniformed man making his way towards me through the haze of dust emanating from my trunk. I coughed.

I could now see that there were two men. One was approaching me and the other was by their vehicle. I thought it best to answer honestly. "Nuthin."

For some reason, my disheveled appearance, bad smell from the bike ride, and the late hour did not help my credibility.

"Oh yeah? Then what's in the bag?" He pointed into the trunk. I could not for the life of me remember what the word for bird-poop was. It's just not a word that comes up much in average conversation. If it does, then maybe you should consider changing your circle of friends.

"Well?"

"It's ... ah ... it's bird uhm ...." The only thing I could think of to do was to mime the word, which did not go over well. It's almost one o'clock in the morning at this point, and here I am, trying to mime the word for 'bird doo-doo' to a cop who's got grandiose dreams of some big drug bust. While they're glaring at me, and lighting me up with their flashlights like I'm on centre stage, I start flapping my arms, and making cooing sounds. Then I make the motion that something is coming out of my behind. What would you do?

"Don't be a wise guy with me. WHAT'S IN THE BAG?"

Panic.

"I'm trying to tell you. It's ...."

Again I start walking in circles, cooing, flapping my arms and making the butt motion. This was like waving a red flag at an already enraged bull.

"Gahh!" The impatient officer pushed past me and made for the trunk. His partner closed ranks and loosened his holster.

Gulp.

The good officer reached into the bag, pulled out a handful of powder, and took a big ole smell.

"Ack!" He sputtered and dropped the rest, making a cloud of dust. "It's bird shit!"

I dared not laugh. Besides, his partner was laughing more than enough for both of us.

When things calmed down, with the officer having coughed and spat all he wanted to, I tried to explain that that was what I was trying to mime. This only caused another round of roars from his partner which did nothing to placate the man I was dealing with.

"What's your name?"

"Erik Gingles."

"Jingles?" he says with a touch of sarcasm.

"That's right. Like Jingle Bells" I hate saying that, but it's the easiest way for people to get it. I suppose if I took a snort of pigeon dung, I'd be a little sarcastic too.

"I.D.?"

Being dressed the way I was, I didn't have any, but was able to produce the car's registration and insurance papers which seemed to satisfy them somewhat at least to the ownership of the car. They had no interest in seeing where I had dumped the first load of contraband, so with a stern warning not to fertilize after midnight, as it disturbed the neighbours, I was allowed to go.

I never returned. Caroline's busy schedule kept her away from the mangy plot for the rest of the summer as well. All that excitement for nothing. But on more than one occasion, while driving by in our car, Caroline has commented that she found it odd that some of the weeds in the corner were growing much higher than the rest.

"Oh really?" I'd say. "I wonder why?"

Society

The Man on the Hill

Note: For those of you not in the mood, I feel I should warn you that the following is a serious chapter. Not all things are laughable and one such incident I think should be included. It affected me just as much or maybe even more, in some ways, as did all the other things that have happened over the years. This event reiterated for me that life can be all too short, and small problems are made far too serious.

In another month and a half it will be six years since it happened, but it seems much longer now. In February of that year, I decided to go for a ride up in the mountains. Each narrow valley shooting off the main Shinshu valley seemed to have its own distinct look about it. On this warm day I wanted to go to the top of a mountain pass I had been eyeing for some time.

For the most part the gravel road leading up this narrow valley was clear of snow. Occasionally there were patches of ice to contend with, but by and large this was not a problem. The clouds were dark and heavy with some low-lying fog patches adding to the general gloominess of the day. The narrow road wound its way up and followed the path of a small river which was making its way down.

There wasn't much noise besides the sound of running

water and the heavy panting of my labouring up the steep pitches. As I got higher, the snow on the road became a little deeper, and I was glad to see that someone had already been up the road in their car. Riding in the tire tracks made going a lot easier and I assumed the tracks were made by the mushroom pickers who occasionally made a day of it in the mountains.

Up and up I went, with my head down, carefully following the ruts made by the tires. Every now and again I'd look up to make sure I wasn't riding to the edge of a cliff and to keep an eye open for any stray boulders falling onto the road with the melting of the snow. It was on one of these glimpses up that things changed for me a little bit for the rest of my life.

I had my head off the handlebars just long enough to look ahead about twenty metres. In my peripheral vision, I noticed a pair of feet on the top of an embankment overlooking the road. Raising my head further to issue a "Hello," I then noticed that the feet weren't touching the ground. It seemed the person I thought was someone out for a day of picking mushrooms had a much less pleasant purpose in mind.

I thought my eyes must have been mistaken and looked again. The second set of signals to my brain confirmed the first. This man, this stranger on the hill, had taken his own life with a simple yellow nylon rope tied around his neck and to a thin branch that didn't look like it could hold the weight of the snow that was on it. It was the kind of rope you can buy at any hardware store for a quarter a metre. With this, he ended what God had given.

I just stood there astraddle my bike and stared. It suddenly occurred to me that he could still be alive, but one look at his face told me that was not the case. There was no sound. Nothing at all. I couldn't hear the sound of the small brook anymore, nor even the slightest sound of a breeze. Nothing. So I yelled at him.

For no reason that is clear to me, I yelled at him. I yelled that he was an idiot for doing what he did. I yelled at him for the pain that he would be causing his family. I yelled that he was a selfish bastard because now he was affecting me and getting me involved with something I had no idea about. I even yelled at him for ruining my ride.

After that, I was at a loss as to what to do. What do you do?

His car was there. It was a mid-sized, nondescript sedan. Grey to match the clouds. I got off my bike and leaned it against a tree on the side of the road. For some reason I felt there would be some explanation for his suicide in his car. Something that would explain what I couldn't imagine. Even though I knew I couldn't read anything that might be there, I still wanted to look.

While keeping an eye on the man on the hill, I slowly walked over to his car. I don't know what I was expecting him to do, but I couldn't help looking over at him. It struck me that if he were to move, I'd probably drop dead right then and there myself.

In the car the keys were left on the front seat. My feelings of there being some explanation for what he did in the car were proven correct. Scattered all over the inside were endless pieces of paper with scrawlings all over them. Receipts from convenience stores, the back of advertisement flyers, parking stubs and old newspapers. Anything that would hold the ink of pen had the last desperate words of the man on the hill.

It was all written haphazardly and hurriedly in Japanese. I couldn't understand a thing. I couldn't make any sense out of why he did what he did. I felt he owed it to me, but I wasn't to get any answers. One piece of paper however, had something I could understand. The time and the date. Feb. 12th, eleven-thirty a.m.

I looked at my watch. It was two-twenty in the afternoon on Feb. 12th. I had missed him by less than three hours.

All kinds of thoughts swept through my mind. What if I

had been here sooner? What if I had started my ride earlier as I had originally planned? What if I was here when he was getting ready or had just done it? I could have saved him. I could have stopped him. I was probably the only other person up on this mountain and I wasn't there when I should have been. I felt helpless. I felt that I had been his only chance, and I let him down, and that made me feel guilty. More guilty than I have ever felt before. I know I didn't have a reason to feel that way, but I did. There was no one else there besides me.

Then I got angry again. Angry at someone I didn't know, who was making me feel this way without saying a word.

Fairly soon the sky was going to get darker than it already was and I didn't want to be up there any longer. Someone had to be told.

Turning my bike around I headed back down the hill. There were some young guys I had seen earlier monkeying around by the river near the base of the mountain. Maybe I'd tell them. But I didn't know what to say. All this time I kept thinking that I was the only one who knew that there was a dead person hanging from a tree just two hundred metres behind me. And it was information I didn't want to keep to myself.

My mind was racing as to what to do.

At the bottom of the mountain I turned left onto the main road in the area. Every little town or hamlet like the one I was in had a local police box. In such places, there is usually just one officer, who lives there with his family. It was there that I went to play a very dark game of charades.

It was now late afternoon. I knocked on the door and went in. Just inside the door is a small entrance way with a counter and bell. I rang it once, then twice. A young officer, not much older than I was, came into the room behind the counter, from what I guessed was his kitchen. He still had a napkin tucked into his shirt and was wiping his hands. I apologized for disturbing him.

Six years ago my Japanese was non-existent. It was a struggle to say hello, let alone try and explain what I had to. There was no other option, so I began.

On the wall, there was a detailed map of the area. I mimed that I was riding my bicycle (showed him my bike through the window), and had gone up this valley on the left-hand side of the map. I went on to say what I had seen. He just looked at me with a big question mark over his forehead. I tried again.

Over and over I was motioning that someone was hanging from a tree. I kept pretending that something was around my neck and that I was hanging, and then would point at the map. By this time his wife had come out and was watching the show. Now both of them were beside me staring in silence while I went through the motions. Looking back on it now, it seems funny, the thought of the two of them standing side by side watching me, taking turns saying what they thought it was I was trying to say. Finally, he got it.

After maybe the sixth or eighth try his eyes opened wide and he nodded his head that he understood and ran off to make a phone call. I was now freezing as it had been raining a bit and I didn't have any rain gear with me. The young officer's wife kindly invited me into the room behind the counter and sat me in front of their space heater. She disappeared for a few moments and then came back into the room with some hot tea and biscuits. They didn't last long.

Next, her husband came back in and explained in a painfully long amount of time through an English-Japanese dictionary, that police officers had to come from town and would be about thirty minutes in getting to where we were. As I was the only one who knew where to go, they asked if I could wait. So I did.

It was a very long thirty minutes. The three of us just sat and waited, not really being able to talk to one another. After forty minutes the other officers arrived. With a few introductions and a brief account of what happened, we all headed out in a four-car motorcade with lights flashing.

Up the mountain we went. It seemed so different now. Every corner and fallen rock seemed so familiar. Especially the last corner before we got there. As we rounded that, the top of the headlights caught the bottom part of the man on the hill's legs. All four cars stopped suddenly and there was a brief moment of silence as everyone took in the scene. Then it was down to business.

Four men scrambled up the embankment and went to work on getting him down. The thick underbrush made it a little difficult. So did the steep slope of the embankment down to the road. While two grabbed the man's legs and hoisted him up a bit, the other ones cut the rope. The sudden shift in weight caused the two holding onto his legs to lose their balance. Their feet slipped in the earth as they slid down the knoll. In doing so, they lost their grip on the man and he fell to the ground and rolled the four metres to the road. Right by where I was standing.

I wanted to go home.

The officers sheepishly scurried down the embankment and straightened him out and went for the body bag. With a little effort they got him in, quite literally threw him into the back of the van, and headed off down the mountain. Another officer (the one I had first met), drove the man's car back while the rest and I took the other cars.

Once back at the small station there was little ceremony, and they were soon off with their silent ward. It was now back to the young officer, his wife and me.

They insisted on driving me home, but I was more insistent on riding. It was dark, but I had a good light and really needed the time to think. They finally relented and agreed to let me go home alone. Before I left, the officer and his wife both disappeared into their living quarters and came back with some things for me to take in lieu of a reward. His missus gave me a container of homemade pickles, and the officer gave me a full bottle of brandy. I guess he thought I could use it. And he was right.

I thanked them for their kindness and asked to make a call to Caroline before I left, as she was probably quite worried that I wasn't home yet. I then made the call and had to assure Caroline that I was indeed fine (much better than the other guy), and would really rather make my own way home. I would tell her everything when I got back.

It took a long time for me to come to terms with what I had seen. At night for a long time I would see his face when I closed my eyes. But as with all things, time slowly wears away those images. Exactly one year later, I went back up the mountain on Feb. 12th and laid an orange on the site as they do in Japan on grave markers. I said a prayer, read a poem my mother had written about the incident, and went home.

On the way back, I went past the police box to say hello and to return the container that the pickles came in, but the young officer had been transferred and the new guy had absolutely no idea what I was talking about. I told him it was nothing and left. A sense of closure, I guess.

From that point on, I've tried not to take things that upset me too seriously, and I never rode on that mountain again.

The Three R's
Readin', Ritin', and Recyclin'

Recycling in Japan is a way of life that borders on fanaticism. Young children are taught from an early age to separate their tins from their aluminums. This is a good thing. But any good thing in excess can be bad.

All garbage must be separated. In our kitchen, which like most is pretty tiny, we have three large plastic garbage cans. One for plastics, one for cans, and one for regular burnable stuff. A pile in the corner is for newspapers and cardboard. All of this together takes up a large chunk of our floor space, but we don't mind because it's for the good of the environment.

On the appropriate day, according to the schedule that the city delivers to your door at the beginning of each new year, you can leave recyclables on a designated curb. Things that don't fit into your bins, like clothes, beds, bicycles and TVs, are referred to as *sodai* (big) garbage. They are to be taken to the designated dropoff spot in your neighbourhood once a month and only on the times printed on the schedule for that day.

Like most things organized in Japan, this system is highly evolved. Neighbourhoods are divided into groups. They are communally responsible for many aspects of their neighbourhood maintenance, from cutting and weeding grass in the local playground, to night patrols to make sure no one is lurking around who shouldn't be. Members, among which we are, have to take turns doing the various tasks, one of which is to get up at five a.m. to organize the large *sodai* garbage. The city will take pretty much anything, but it's got to be on the right day according to the schedule. (God help you if you get caught putting your cans out the night before). Newspapers must be stacked and tied with a string. The paper milk and juice containers must be washed, the bottoms cut out for easy folding, and the plastic spout removed, and then tied in bundles. The cans must be separated into aluminum and tin categories. If all of these instructions are not carried out to a 'T,' you'll be set upon by the Garbage Gestapo and be beaten on the bottoms of your feet with an old boot, properly laced of course.

The rule of thumb is that all things must be flattened and tied, except clothing, which has to be folded as well. You'll get a smile if you iron them before you take them to the curb. The tying of everything is actually annoying and redundant, for as soon as you hand everything over all neatly wrapped as if for Christmas, it's immediately cut open right in front of you and then dumped into a large container.

"What's the point," you ask?

Ah ha! You've still haven't figured it out yet, have you my friend? For many things, there doesn't seem to be a point. It just IS.

Six years ago the garbage that we put on the curb every week, like everyone else's was in old plastic grocery-store bags. This seemed like a logical thing to do, re-using those nasty bags that tended to multiply under our kitchen sink. But the Garbage Gestapo couldn't see into those bags and check if the good people of the city were really environmentally conscious, or whether they were trying to slip a few cans in with the orange peels. So, the city government decided to crack down on this potential insurrection and passed an edict that all the citizens of Matsumoto must now buy and use see-through blue plastic bags. This allowed the authorities to keep an eye on things.

At that time, there were green see-through bags on the market, but for some reason they weren't acceptable. Anybody caught blatantly using the green bags, would run the risk of having a chicken nailed to their door in the middle of the night. We asked the volunteers at the dropoff if we could use up the green ones we had.

"No," was the answer.

And that was that.

Not wanting to be the nail that sticks up only to be hammered down, we started using the blue bags. Things got back to normal. The neighbours breathed a little easier. A routine had been re-established … or so we thought.

Fascism doesn't happen overnight. Oh no. It happens slowly, bit by bit, until it's too late to turn back the tide on what was once normalcy. History repeats itself. Unfortunately, no one bothers to keep the old programs. First, introduce some recycling ideas for the good of the masses. Next, do away with the grocery store bags and bring out the blue ones. Soon, those who continue to use the green ones don't show up for work one day. They can't be reached by family or friends. No answer on the telephone or at the door. Soon, there's a little unrest from the people and *Wham!* out come the Brownshirts with their new plan to cow the renegade recyclers and bring a new order to town.

Notices were circulated that, as of the first of March 1996, everyone must report to City Hall to pick up their own clear plastic bags that have a white square with a rough surface so you can write your name on your garbage. Can you imagine?

The bit about nailing the chicken to your door was admittedly a figment of my imagination, but the autographed garbage is a fact. This could be a little embarrassing for some people who may have unusual habits. I mean, having their garbage out there in a clear plastic bag, with their name written all over it?

"Whooaaa. Look at that Yamamoto San. Up to his old tricks again, I see, that ole scally-wag."

Invasion of privacy perhaps? I can't imagine that a few pieces of paper getting into the regular garbage is that much of a problem, or that the municipal government has to be a purveyor of everyone's waste. It would be, however, a good way to get back at someone if you were the revengeful kind.

"Zo! We've been watching you Yamamoto San, yah! Vat have you done vit za tin cans yah?"

"I swear I have no idea how those cans got into the regular garbage! Someone must have put my name on their bag!"

"You know vee don't take too kindly to people who don't take our reziclink program zeriously. Take heem avay! Two more weeks for za Reziclink thought-educazion!"

Of course, I keep all of these thoughts to myself and dutifully put our name on our bag. I also look the other way if someone is set upon by black-clad storm trooopers and whisked away into an all-white van, never to be seen at the curb on garbage day again.

Such recycling militancy, though extreme, serves a purpose. On this skinny, elongated island, roughly 25% of the land is suitable for cultivation or habitation. With 125,000,000 people (half the U.S.) crammed into a total land mass a little smaller than the state of Montana, waste disposal becomes a very large issue. But herein lies a paradox. The average Japanese item bought at any given department store is wrapped a total of 126 times. Let's use a pair of men's briefs as an example. The original item comes in a box. Then, there's the store's box which the original box goes into. Then there is wrapping around the outer box. It's then put into a paper bag with handles. This ensemble then goes into a box the size of a floor model TV, filled with styrofoam peanuts, shrink-wrapped and then delivered by a refrigerated tractor-trailer to your door. Sorry. You can stop at the wrapped box being put into a larger paper bag part.

The word 'excessive' comes to mind. If you buy a box of cookies, the cookies are individually wrapped in that plastic-like tin foil, which in turn are set into a plastic tray which is in a larger plastic-like tin foil covering, which is put in another bag etc., etc., etc. Refusing a bag or a box at the cash register of a large department store is good way to cause some form of panic. The cashier looks around nervously and starts to fidget. Some look like they're about to cry. It makes you feel guilty, but for the good of the environment you must be strong.

Another thing that tends to add to the necessity of such fanatic recycling is that the Japanese are perhaps some of the biggest consumers you've ever seen. New is best. Anything outdated, (over five years old) is quickly replaced. This includes all the big-ticket items like TVs, stereos, VCRs, washers and heaters. Much of this stuff is hauled off to the *sodai* garbage spot at some time or another. The designated dropoff area becomes a kind of free outdoor market for the new foreigners in town. In the early years a friend snagged a refrigerator which just needed a little cleaning. We picked up a 21" colour TV and a propane heater. Nothing wrong with any of it.

At first you're shocked that the stuff is being thrown away. Then you feel a little disgusted with yourself that you're actually entertaining ideas of rooting through someone else's garbage. But then you go to a store and see how much this 'garbage' costs new. The very next month you find yourself putting a balaclava over your face and heading down to the *sodai gomi* dropoff zone with flashlight in hand and using code names like 'Tango' and 'Charley' for each other as you raid the depot.

Don't feel bad though. It's all part of that circle of life called 'recycling' and the Garbage Gestapo will thank you for it.

Used Tires

Pretty much the only thing that really needs to be replaced on a second-hand car is the tires. There are many places where you can get used tires for about 80% less than the original price. These tires, like the cars, appear never to have been used. The tires I picked up from the used-tire lot still had those little rubber whiskers down the centre.

I was looking to get winter tires and hoped to get a little salvage rebate from the summer ones that came with my car. The auto mechanic shop attached to the factory where I work said they'd give me 1000 yen each (ten dollars) for my old tires. I thanked them and said I'd think about it. Being a prudent business man, I didn't want to jump at the first offer that came along. I decided to talk to the old guy who ran a huge scrap yard not too far away.

Having arrived at the junk yard and standing face to face with the proprietor, it was clear to me that this weathered-looking little man was definitely not into using any skin moisturizers. On this cold, overcast January day, he had his little cap crammed down low over his head and the collar turned up on his greasy coveralls. The only way I could discern where his mouth was, through all those deep wrinkles under the low brim of his hat, was to watch the steam and to follow it to the crevice from whence it came.

He must have spent the better part of the century working outside in the middle of his stacked-tire fortress with an oil drum smoldering away in the centre. I entered the chamber and asked the wizened one how much he'd give me for my tires. We shuffled back to the car. I began the opening salvo of the negotiations.

"So. What do you think? How much?"

The old guy cupped his ear. "What?"

"HOW MUCH FOR THE TIRES!"

"Oh. 1500 yen each."

All right! I made an extra five on each one compared to the original offer at the other place.

"Shop around," I always tell Caroline. "Don't buy from the first place you see. Patience is the key. Research saves you money."

I was wise.

I took the tires out and rolled them to the inner sanctum of the rubber fortress, which was surprisingly warm, and stacked them up. At this point, things began to go askew. I believed in my soul that he was going to pay me for my tires. Later he would sell them to a large tire company to be recycled. The truth was, I had to pay him for the privilege of storing my old tires on his lot. A kind of paid parking place for old tires if you will. Realizing who was the payer and who was the payee took a little longer than it should have.

"So. 1500 times four. That's 6000 yen."

"Yep. That's right. 6000 yen."

Both of us stood around the stack of tires admiring them like some obscure piece of modern art. Each of us waiting for the other one to pull out his wallet and hand over the moolah. The old gent was getting a little agitated and repeated the terms.

"That's 1500 each, right? So that's 6000 yen total."

"That's right, yeah."

"Uh-huh."

"Yyyyep."

We rocked back and forth on our heels and kicked the tires a few times until ole Leatherface couldn't take it any more. "Well?"

"Well, what?"

"Wellll... where's the money?"

"What do you mean, 'Where's the money?'"

Perhaps he thought I was some young punk trying to pull a fast one using the language barrier as an excuse. Perhaps he's had trouble with foreigners in the past, or perhaps he just had gas, but he practically exploded, sending his wrinkles to a tight mass at the top of his face. "What do YOU mean, by 'What do I mean' about 'Where's the money.' Give me the 6000 yen!"

"Give you the 6000 yen! But you're getting the tires!"

"Of course I'm getting the tires!" he squeaked in exasperation.

It was then that I clued in and tried to backpedal.

"But the other shop said they'd only charge me 1000 yen for each."

"Take them back then."

There was little sympathy in his voice and it wasn't worth the hassle, nor the embarrassment of taking them back to the original garage. Besides, I was unsure if this tire scam came under the control of the Garbage Police or not. Tired out, I paid the man and left.

Free Cars and Driving Slippers

Fact. New cars are expensive. In Japan, the minute you drive your new car off the lot it drops in value. And drops big time. I wouldn't be surprised if signs were put up every fifty metres on the side of the road starting at the dealership saying; "Your car's value has now dropped 10% … 20% … 30% … 40% … 50% …" By the time you've reached the first set of traffic lights, you'd be driving a practically worthless, brand new, fully loaded Lexus.

The source of this value-dip information comes from a private car dealer pal of mine. Hence, secondhand cars can be acquired on the cheap. Cars in the seven- or eight-year-old range are often let go for free. There are many reasons why.

Every car must be inspected. A new car's inspection is good for three years. After that point, the inspection has to be carried out every two years. With this inspection sticker, you are allowed to drive your car on the road, as the inspection, called *shaken* (shaw-ken), has the minimum amount of driving coverage insurance included. You have to get a regular car insurance policy for liability and the like, but legally, you can drive the car with just the *shaken*.

Sounds good, eh? The *shaken*, however, costs $1,500 to $2,000 each time it's done. When a car gets older, and the *shaken* has to be done every second year, it becomes impractical to keep it. Junking your car isn't a very attractive alternative either, as you have to pay roughly $1000 just to get rid of it (like the tires). Hence, with second hand cars being next to worthless, though in perfectly good shape, they are often given away to save the $1000 towing charges.

A few months ago, there was a story in the paper that depicted how costly disposing of a large number of cars can be. A university was having a lot of trouble with recent graduates who would abandon their eight- or ten-year-old cars on campus. The graduates would remove their licence plates and walk away. It was costing the university tens of thousands of dollars each year to have them disposed of.

The majority of buyers of these eight- to ten-year-old cars are foreigners who are looking for a cheap mode of transportation. The rest of the cars are gathered up by entrepreneurs and sold to Russia, China and other East Asian countries for a tidy profit. We're not talking Lamborghinis or Jaguars, and you may say "Who wants a ten year old heap anyway?" But before you look a gift car under the hood, let's look at the situation more closely.

First, the average number of kilometres a car is driven in Japan is from five to seven thousand a year, primarily because it's much faster and more convenient to take the train.

Second, some people wear different shoes for driving. To make the switch, they open the car door and sit down bum-first with their feet still outside the car. Next, they remove their regular shoes and pick them up while swinging their feet inside. After that, they put their shoes in a plastic tray under the seat, and then put on their driving shoes which are sitting on a perfectly clean floor mat. This cleanliness extends to the rest of the car. Many people have seat covers which leaves the interior pretty much the way it came out of the showroom. Just like the way some people keep the plastic on a lampshade or sofa.

Third, salt is not used on the roads, so for the most part, the cars don't rust.

Driving shoes are not the only accessory for cars. The little gadgets and knicknacks that can be purchased for one's auto are a huge industry. Some of these include fibre optic dangling lights, car perfume, small TVs that plug into your lighter for when you're really bogged down in traffic, little VCR decks to go along with the TVs, an endless array of goose-neck lamps, multi-headed adapters for your lighter socket to accommodate all these things, seat covers, wireless remote CD players that'll hold up to ten CDs, tiny refrigerators for your back dash, electronic satellite guidance systems, and last but not least, plastic trays for your street shoes.

One of the first times that I was picked up by a friend in Japan, he had already removed his outdoor shoes and had them safely stored under the seat. I was getting into the car, as I had done for years quite successfully when he yelped. "Wait! Your shoes! You forgot you shoes!"

As far as I could tell, I was wearing my shoes and hadn't forgotten them at all. "What are you talking about?"

"You're wearing your outdoor shoes. Please don't wear your shoes in my car."

This confused me. If I didn't wear my shoes, what exactly was I going to do when we got to where we were going?

He leaned under the passenger seat and pulled out a plastic tray that had two-inch-high sides and told me to put my feet in there. The plastic tray he had for his shoes was a nice square, green thing. Mine was a pink, heart-shaped one. Obviously, his passengers were usually women, or so I hoped.

I complied. It was a little uncomfortable as the size of the tray forced me to sit with my knees together in a low-riding bucket seat. The image of myself sitting in a car with my knees pressed together and feet in a pink plastic heart-shaped tray did not fill me with machismo. But he didn't seem to mind. After all, I was doing it for him, the big lug.

Bars and Bottle Keeps

As every salaried office worker must work, so too must he drink.

Alcohol consumption seems to be a rite of passage for younger employees. Older staff members jovially harass newcomers to drink after work. This is not social drinking, but more a test of your liver. And it never really stops. Once you've been with the company long enough to prove you're a team player at the after-work booze-a-thons, it soon becomes your turn the following spring to get the new recruits to play the game. It's an endless circle.

Being a foreigner, I was an exception to the company drinking rule when I joined the team and was mercifully not cajoled into the usual festivities. It could have been my breath. Yet some things are a must for all to attend. One is the section's year-end party (*bonenkai* — literally meaning 'drinking to forget the past year'), which can take place anywhere from mid-November to the end of December. The other biggy, is the section's New Year party (*shininkai*), which takes place anytime from the first of January to the middle of February.

These parties, much like everything else, run like clockwork. If the starting time for an organized party is six o'clock, then the starting time is six o'clock. Not one minute before, nor one minute after. What's good for the starting time is also good for the finishing time. The standard 'drinking party' (that's what they're called) is from six to nine. That's it. At nine, whether you've just opened another bottle or not, you're expected to abandon it and leave the premises.

Granted, if you're having a private party with some friends, you can usually have an extra few minutes to down the rest of your beer, but company parties at a hotel finish exactly on time. No exceptions.

So, with the official company party over rather early, what are you going to do? Well, after the first party many people will divide into smaller groups and go on to their own 'second' party. This party takes place at a different shop than the first. Younger people tend to go to *izakayas* (ee-za-kai-yas) which are a rough equivalent to North American pubs or taverns.

Here, you can order pub-like food such as fried potatoes, fish, tofu, chicken wings, green beans and raw octopus tentacles. Mmmmm good! The food comes on separate plates, and everyone is expected to share. Of course, to wash it down, you can order draught that comes in big frosted, glass mugs. If you aren't up for a draught, you can order bottles of beer. These are of the larger variety (650 ml), and everyone has a small 5 oz. glass placed in front of them. Drinking directly from the bottle is a big no-no. And don't pour for yourself. You fill the glass of the person sitting next to you. In response, they pick up the same bottle and pour for you. If your glass is empty, and no one notices, pick up a bottle and pour them some beer, even if their glass is almost full. This is the hint for them to fill yours up.

The pouring custom is rarely explained to a foreigner. My first time met with predictable results. Three big bottles were placed on the table with five glasses. I assumed that two more bottles were coming and picked up one and starting drinking. All eyes were upon me, wide with shock. Only then was the custom explained. They never poured from my bottle except for me after that.

This system of drinking also makes it very difficult to keep track of how much you've had to drink. Inevitably, someone is always giving you the hint, and your glass is never empty.

"Honest offither, I ... only had one teeney glath."

In *izakayas*, the decor is rustic, with heavy wooden dark tables and chairs. Some have *tatami* mat areas where people can sit on the floor — not so far to fall that way. There are lots of big white plaster walls criss-crossed with big wooden beams. Potted plants and free-standing paper screens make up the rest. There's usually a rough-hewn counter allowing patrons a clear view into the kitchen. This way customers can check if the octopus tentacles are fresh or of the frozen variety. Some places have music blaring Japanese Top Forty tunes, or just plain Japanese Muzak, which is pretty much the same thing to me. The lights are bright and the crowd noisy.

The major difference from a pub back home is that people in Japan stay seated. The number of people in the pub matches the number of occupied chairs. The only time you get up, besides to leave, is to go to the washroom, thereby allowing you a quick scan of the room. There is no mingling. You get the feeling that if you did try to mingle, the music would stop, people would turn their heads with mouths agape, and the guys in the kitchen would come running out from behind the bar screaming something, with their octopus cleavers held aloft.

I don't know this for a fact of course, but it's just a feeling. And it's not something I'd want to test. Besides, I'm married.

So, if you come with a group of friends, stay put, drink from the glass, don't spend too long in the bathroom, and let the good times roll. Bring on the Octopus!

If the younger generation goes to *izakayas* for their second party, the thirty-something and up crowd heads straight for shot bars, or hostess clubs.

At these places, you are likely to find the wall behind the bar filled row upon row with bottles of whiskey. I would hazard a guess that 98% of all hard liquor consumed in Japan is whiskey or bourbon. If you look closely at these bottles, you'll notice that each one has a customer's name tagged to it. They are previously bought and kept for that person's private use. Most men frequent the same bar, or have bottles at two or three different places. This system is called 'Bottle Keeps' and fits in perfectly with that innate sense of belonging to some kind of group. It makes you feel like you are a part of this establishment. Where everybody knows your name. Where everybody is a 'Norm!' san.

It must be the sense of belonging which comes with a bottle keep that keeps people coming back to the same place. From what I can surmise, there is no real financial benefit to it. You're charged around $75 U.S. for a bottle that would cost you $25 U.S. in a store. Every time you go, you're given a pitcher of water, a bucket of ice and stir stick. A night of ice cubes and water over the run of two hours or more, will cost about $200 U.S. Of course, chocolate-coated corn flakes in a dish the size of a small ashtray are also provided. The price for the same amount of drinking at the bar without using your own bottle is about $200 U.S.

At one point in time, I had a bottle keep. It was at an *izakaya* actually, which is not normally a place for such things. It was a present from the pub's manager.

Every Friday night Caroline taught in a village outside of town. For the year and a half that she did that, I would wait for her train at this *izakaya* called 'Inaka' (Countryside) near the station. Sitting at the counter every week allowed me to get to know the staff. I mentioned that I didn't really care for whiskey, but that rum was more my kind of drink. A staple of bars on the East Coast at home. One Friday while sitting in my regular spot, I was proudly presented with my very own bottle of rum, all set to go, with my name written incorrectly, yet lovingly, on the tag. I was touched. The manager waved off my many thanks with embarrassment and said it was the least he could do for such a valued customer.

I ordered about three glasses of cola to go with my rum over the next hour and a half. I figured on my way to the cash register, that with the free rum, and only three glasses of cola, plus the fried potatoes and tofu, I'd be in for about 1500 yen ($15 U.S).

Surprise!

My 'free' rum cost me 3200 yen ($32 U.S.).

"Waddya mean 3200 yen! I thought the rum was a gift?"

"It is a gift, but the cola costs 700 yen a glass."

"Seven hundred yen a glass? But a big bottle of beer only costs 500 yen."

"That's right."

He reached over and took the money from my hand.

There is a saying in Japan — "There is nothing more expensive than a free gift."

Ain't it the truth?

For the most part, hostess bars or snacks (as they are sometimes called), are where the majority of bottle keeps are kept. A hostess bar, as the name implies, is a bar where paid hostesses are attending the customers. The places are usually small, and there are literally thousands of them in different areas around the train station. Many of them are roughly 7 by 8 metres and can squeeze in twenty people on a Friday night. The seats are usually covered in crushed red velvet and the lights are low.

To attend the customers are three or four female companions. The word 'waitress' is not really appropriate, as their job is to join you and your party in whatever conversation is going. This was traditionally the job of a geisha. Geishas however were women trained in the art of conversation and poetry, and who were highly skilled in more than a few different musical instruments. They were cultured and refined entertainers with years of rigid training. Gone are the instruments, kimonos and in-depth conversation. Now, it's just chit-chat with girls in usually tight, short skirts and high heels. In some places they only wear lingerie. And you can pay through the nose for it.

It doesn't seem to make much sense really. I mean, it doesn't take a genius from Gaul to figure out that the male to female ratio, if that's what you're going for, is not in your favour. However, it is a guaranteed way for a shy guy to talk to women. Better yet, an even better place to meet women would be a host bar. The same thing, but in this case, a few guys are working the floor serving a room full of young office ladies. Sounds good in theory, but before you go out and buy tickets to come over, they say that men customers aren't allowed in host bars. Yet women can go into hostess bars. Double standards can work both ways.

Another double standard is pricing. Depending on the kind of place you go into, and who you are, the rates vary. For example, if you go to a regular hostess bar, or snack, the girls wear suits that are snug and relatively short with stiletto heeled shoes. The decor is reasonably tasteful and the lights are low. They light your cigarettes and pour the drinks. The conversation is pleasant, and sometimes a few snippets of risqué talk enters in. Naturally, the bar has a karaoke machine, and the hostess will readily agree (though their expression may show otherwise) to singing duets with bleary-eyed, business-suited customers. Two hours or more of this kind of fun will cost the aforementioned $150 to $200 U.S. Split four ways, it's livable for those used to it. To the novice, it's a bit much. In some snacks, they'll charge customers they determine as 'undesirables' several hundred dollars in service charges (honestly), to discourage them from coming back. As owning a drinking establishment does not require a liquor licence, they can charge whatever they want to whoever they want.

If this relaxed atmosphere is not what you're looking for, men can go to a different kind of hostess bar, more like a cabaret or club. Keep an eye on your watch and bring your bank card. In this situation, time is money. At these clubs, you are charged by the hour. The cabarets have dance shows on a small stage. The dancers are usually Thai or Filipino girls and are said to be quite good. These places will charge around $60 an hour and up ... each! But it's all you can drink within that time. Being able to drink, and having a drink from which to drink from, are two different things.

Once seated, hostesses will join you at your table to watch the show. They regulate the flow of drinks, which are painfully slow in coming. Whiskey and water are the only drinks going and there is a heavy emphasis on the water. In a cabaret the atmosphere is more rowdy and the talk a little less genteel. A little touching of the thigh, placing an arm around someone's shoulder and occasionally copping a feel is acceptable and expected, but not necessarily appreciated. The decor is also quite different from the tamer snacks. It's kind of like a disco with no dance floor (except for the tiny stage). There's lots of loud music and you have to shout to be heard. The ratio of men to women is for the most part, one to one, but you're paying for it.

Once after a dinner party, I went to one of these clubs. It was my first, and I can tell you, last time. It was as I had described. We were seated at a booth in a boy-girl-boy-girl kind of arrangement and I felt a little silly paying someone to talk to me. Back home we'd call that 'sad.' Not only that, it seemed these girls were more trained in the art of thigh grabbing than the art of conversation. Fortunately the blaring music and twirling lights filled in the gaps of our discourse.

In an hour's time, one of the girls got up and went to check with the manager or Mama San. When she returned, she asked us if we wanted to stay for another hour. I was such an innocent.

"How much was the first hour?"

"63,000 yen." ($600 U.S.)

I refused to panic.

"Did you say 63,000 yen?"

"That's right. Are you staying another hour?"

I sat there smiling benignly for a few seconds, as a thousand thoughts rushed through my head. "They don't know who I am. They're wearing high heels. They couldn't catch me if they tried. Run!"

I didn't. With an air to my voice of "This place bores me" I responded. "No ... I don't think so. We've a few more places to go."

We got up, paid, and casually left.

Do not get the idea that we were considered 'undesirables' (Heaven forbid) because of the amount we had to fork over. I believe in my heart that we were very desirable, but that is the price you pay for such a high ratio of men to women and a little thigh grabbing.

Once outside and out of earshot, the cussing and accusations began over whose bright idea it was to go in the first place. There were six of us, so it cost $105 each for one hour. I remembered a time, not so long ago, that if I had $105 in the bank I thought I was flush. And now, here I was dropping it down in one hour of watered-down drinking. That's me. Big spender. Living the high life in the Far East.

Seven bucks for a glass of cola was seeming a little more reasonable after that.

Onsens

It is true that most people in Japan are into going to the public bath. Nothing wrong with that really. It's good to be clean. Just ask any commuter on the Tokyo subway squashed up against someone else on a nice warm summer's day.

Not so long ago, having your own bath in your house was unheard of, let alone a shower. Everyone went to the local bath house to scrub down. Many little rituals evolved from neighbours getting naked and bathing together. Like forming a line and washing each others backs (true), and also more recently, the uncanny resurgence of traditional Greco-Roman wrestling (not true).

Nowadays, almost everyone has their own shower/bath combo in their abode. Yet bath houses with their variety of baths at different temperatures, steam rooms and saunas, maintain their popularity. In today's fast-paced world, there's nothing more relaxing than taking off all your clothes and jumping into a tub full of naked strangers. Now that's livin'!

Not all bath houses are the same. There are two basic types: *onsens* have natural thermogeo heat, and *sentos*, are heated by furnaces. Each kind of bathhouse has tubs in a variety of styles, shapes and temperatures. Some tubs are quite shallow and have reclining stone seats. Others have the bather sit upright, as if in a straight back chair, up to the top of your chest in water, while more hot water pours down like an endless tongue onto your shoulders. Some baths have a current of electricity running through them. What for, I have no idea, but there you are.

Some baths are even outside in a stone garden, where the water flows in through a bamboo pipe nestled in the cedar trees. The serenity of the gentle setting, coupled with the soothing effects of the tension-letting hot water, lulls the bather into a blissful state of tranquillity. And yet, for the uninitiated foreigner, the whole time you are in this place of total relaxation, you are constantly aware that you are sitting next to a person you don't know, of the same sex, and you're both naked.

For North Americans, such baths and spas are not so common. Hence, going to a *sento* or *onsen* for the first time can be a little unnerving. Getting into a hot tub with naked strangers and not being paid for it, had not originally been my idea of a good time. Admittedly, before I came to Japan, I didn't like sushi either, but I do now. Things change. You mature as an adult. Before I knew it, I was buck naked in a tankful of people I didn't know and lovin' it.

Bath houses do not consist only of baths. There are shower stalls surrounding the outside walls so you can shower before you get into the tub. Much in the same way that you wash the dishes before you put them into the dishwasher. Actually this is a good thing because who would want to get into a tub of someone else's greasy water. *Ewww.*

I guess the word 'stall' in the term 'shower stall' is inappropriate. There are no dividers between the shower nozzles. In fact, there is only a little plastic stool to squat on in front of a mirror, accompanied by a little plastic wash basin. The shower attachment is a hand-held job that is secured to the wall at waist level. Most places provide soap and shampoo. There's usually a communal drinking cup hanging somewhere from the wall to use when the heat gets to be too much. I have yet to see someone use it.

Once you get used to the whole scene, it really is relaxing

and enjoyable. There are however, two things that I still don't care for. The first being that the person who usually takes the money at the entrance way is quite often able to see into both changing rooms.

This can be rather unnerving if an older woman is sitting on an elevated chair behind a counter and watching you undress. I suppose it is no less pleasant for a female when a man is sitting on the chair and can see into the women's room. They try to make it look like they're not really watching. They have the decency of pretending to watch a strategically located TV. But if you look at them closely, their eyes are shooting past the TV and into the change room of choice.

No one I've mentioned this to seems to think this set-up odd, yet most people tend to undress around corners if possible, or under towels.

The other thing that is not my cup of tea falls under the same 'staff' category. It's the cleaning women. They are just that. Women. Rarely do you see a cleaning man. These women come bustling in and out of the *sento* during business hours. They wear rubber boots, dish washing gloves, replace the soap, and generally, have a peek.

It was during one of their little excursions into the men's side that I was made to feel a little uncomfortable.

I can't recall my first experience in a public bath, but by this time in my tenure, I had become quite acclimatized to *onsens* and the like. It really is a great way to relax, soaking in hot water up to your neck on a cold winter's day, especially at night in the outside tubs called *ofuros* set in Japanese gardens. There's nothing like hunkering down in the water with your wash cloth on your head as the snow gently falls past the subdued flood lights in the trees and disappears without a sound in the hot water all around you. This day was different.

It was a cold spring at a mountain bike race far away from home. I was freezing after having camped and raced in the mud. Most races are held at ski hills where the lodge has a massive *onsen*, and oh, how inviting this one looked on that cold day.

I stripped the mud-caked jersey off my shivering pale body. I put it, and my cycling shorts, into a plastic bag and then put that into the wicker basket provided on the shelf. I grabbed my little wash cloth, and holding it in front of me, as one does, made my way to the door in the centre of the huge steamed-up window. I could smell the almost boiling water and my quivering limbs and numb feet were begging me to hurry. Then, out of nowhere, she came.

Just as I was about to open the door, a voice from behind me spoke.

"Excuse me!"

I turned.

There standing in front of me was one of the cleaning women in her rubber boots, smock and dish washing gloves. I was immediately aware of two things. One, she must have been looking at my tookus. Two, this little hand towel, was indeed little and was no longer adequate for its new function as a cloaking device. Not being one to converse in the nude with older women wearing rubber boots and gloves, I was taken aback.

"Uh, I'm sorry?"

"Where are you from?"

"Canada."

My wishing that my wash cloth would turn into a beach towel was not materializing, so with a polite nod, I made for the door.

"Oh Canada! How lovely. Where in Canada?"

I couldn't believe it. Didn't she know that I was not dressed properly to talk to a lady?

"The East Coast." I said this while backing towards the door and reaching for the handle which led to the steamy sanctuary of the *onsen*. She would not be put off so easily.

For every one step backward I made, she took one forward. I felt so vulnerable. So alone. I wanted to shout, "What the hell's the matter with you? I'm trying to take a bath here!" But I didn't. I wouldn't want anyone yelling at my mother who was just trying to be friendly and bridge that gap of international communication. Then I thought, just what in the heck would my mother be doing in the men's side of the *onsen* anyway? It appeared to be a no-win situation. I continued to squirm, and she smiled.

"Oh the East Coast. I'd love to go to the East Coast."

I just smiled back, and at that moment, I could have sworn that I saw her eyes, just for a fraction of a second, glance down to my reproductive area.

A-ha! I knew it. She was trying to catch a peek! But what should I do? Yell? Blow a whistle? Shout 'Help!' at the top of my lungs? Fire? I think not.

I was an adult male, not to be frightened or made to feel cheap by a member of the opposite sex. I would stand my ground. If challenged, I should meet the challenge head on (no pun intended). Perhaps I should just drop the towel and let her have a look if that is what she really wanted. It's probably just the game she likes, and if I was to make a move to drop the cloth, she'd probably shriek and run away. So, why couldn't I do it?

Perhaps it was a repeat of a problem I had in university. This is not to say that I was being harassed by older rubber-booted women with washing gloves in school. But rather, by a big lummox of a friend.

I have this 230-pound friend, Chris, who, when he got inebriated, liked to try and kiss me. I can't flatter myself by saying that I'm the only guy he tried to kiss. He tried to kiss his roommate and a few other lucky guys. He'd like to grab my face with his big, meaty paws and say in a weak German accent, "I want to kiss you full on za lips," and then try. The kicker for him was to watch me contort and squirm trying to get away.

This continued for more than a year at inopportune times. Finally, his roommate, who was subjected to the same harassment, had had enough. One night at a crowded rough-and-tumble kind of pub, he made his move.

When the inevitable shenanigans started up, the roommate (Lyndon), grabbed Chris on either side of his head and gave him a big kiss, full on za lips for real. And that, my friends, was that. Chris was frozen in terror as all those nearby looked on with raised eyebrows. When he did finally move, he picked up his coat and without another word, made for the door. Subsequently, he never publicly bothered his roommate, or myself, again. A brave and calculated move on Lyndon's part, but not without its share of risks. In the back of my mind I thought, "What if Chris really does want to kiss me. Then where would I be?" It gives me the heebie-jeebies just to think of it.

With this doubt in mind, I was unable to take the risk and drop the wash cloth in hopes of frightening her away. She continued to play the game, but was a little more devious. Eyes poised and ready to peek, she played her trump card.

"So … where did you camp?"

"Over there …."

I instantly realized, as my towel-holding arm instinctively went up to point, that she was waiting for this exact reaction. The cunning. But I was better.

In one fluid movement, I deftly switched towel hands without exposing a thing and pointed to the far parking lot with my unoccupied hand. Just as quick as her eyes glistened in the moments before victory, so too did they dull in the instant of defeat. She was good, but not good enough. With that, I wished her a good day and quickly backed into the *onsen* and was enveloped by the steam. She did not follow.

The day was mine.

Courtesy: A Way of Life

One thing I like about living in Japan is the common courtesy you receive and see in every aspect of life. Many people from around the world experienced it during the Olympics. I don't mean like pulling out a chair for someone or opening a door, but other things. Perhaps it's not so much courtesy, but more of a general philosophy: Be polite. When you enter a store, salesclerks say, or even yell, "Thanks for coming." And when you leave, you get the same message. I know that many part-time store employees probably really don't care if people come in or not. As for me, I'm probably more trouble than I'm worth, but it's still nice to hear someone say, "Thanks. We appreciate you coming," even if it's not from the heart.

This civility permeates all aspects of daily life. I was once driving down a narrow street one night with my Dad who had come to visit. As with many of the side streets in town, they're windy and about one car width, with walls and houses pressed up against the edge of the asphalt. We rounded one corner and there on the street were three twelve-year-old boys who had just lit off a string of firecrackers. It was summer and this sort of thing happens all over.

As they had just set the bunch off and there was no way to put them out, we had to stop and wait about eight to ten seconds while the string danced and flashed around the street. When the last one popped, the boys quickly ran out and stomped on any burning embers. Next, they stepped to the side of the road, doffed their baseball caps, bowed and shouted an apology for delaying us as we drove past. I didn't think too much of it, but Dad's flabber was ghasted.

"What did they say?"

I thought this a prime chance to have him on, but I didn't. "They were apologizing for having held us up."

"You're kidding."

"Nope."

"Can you imagine that …."

We drove on in silence for a while as Dad came to grips with the reality that somewhere in the world polite youngsters still existed.

The silence was short lived when we got on to a major thoroughfare. It was time for Dad to experience gas stations. I thought he was ready.

I would like to point out that there are very few, to no, self-serve gas stations. They're all full service, and given the price of gas, they should be.

When you enter the station, shouts of welcome come from all directions. You feel as if you've accidentally wandered into an F-1 racing pit. Quite often there are three to four men, all in pressed uniforms complete with cap and bow tie, literally running to your car and swarming all over it. Two attendants immediately start wiping your windows with a cloth, while another gets your gas going. A different man asks you if he can empty your ashtray or take any of your garbage. Whichever of the two guys doing your windows is finished first, runs to the driver's side and asks you to pop the hood. He then goes about checking every stick, plunger or connection, real or imaginary, saying everything he's checking out loud for you to hear. The other window-washer helps by repeating everything out loud to double check nothing was missed. The fella emptying your garbage is now back and asks you to pump your brake pedal once or twice to make sure it's in working order.

When all is completed, the windows cleaned, gas tank full, all functioning parts checked, you're given your change and a small packet of tissues. The last act of service is for the attendant to wade in and stop the traffic, allowing you to enter the flow. After you've successfully gotten back onto the road, you can look into your rear-view mirror and see the attendant taking off his hat and bowing to the car that had stopped to let you out.

Like night and day it is, when I think of that little morose, pimply-faced kid who used to work at the gas station around the corner from my mom's house. The only time you'd have gotten him out of his Plexiglas-car-magazine-reading chamber to stop the traffic would have been if his skateboard somehow mysteriously rolled into the street.

This is a nice way to live (not in a Plexiglas box, but in Japan). If it rains and you're out, neighbours will actually take your laundry in. If you let someone into traffic ahead of you, they'll flash their hazards to say 'Thanks.' It's nice.

The only time I don't care for it is at the McDonald's hamburger place by our house. Yes, I do go there occasionally, when the hankering for a double cheeseburger must be met. It usually happens later at night when this particular McDonalds is relatively empty and quiet. As the rule book apparently states, the staff is to thank the customer on the way out. If they are not so busy, a large group is thus available to shout their thanks in unison. I should be used to it by now, but every time I turn my back to the counter and head for the door, they all shout.

"THANKYOUVERYMUCH!"

I think they've got a bet going to see if they can make me drop my food. I can't blame them really. In high school we used to drive around in my Dad's Chev Imapala, playing a rousing game of 'Drop Bag.' You know, where you'd sneakily drive up close to people along the curb and then scream at the top of your lungs to see who could make somebody drop something. But that was different. We weren't getting paid to do it. We did it for the love of the sport.

The last thing I want to mention on the topic of courtesy is the respect that people have for other people's property. This is something I think we should all take note of. There is no greater demonstration of this than the common vending machine. Yes indeed. They're everywhere in Japan. I was told that it takes the energy of one nuclear power plant to run all the vending machines in the country, and I believe it.

For the most part, they're all outside. I don't mean outside a store under bright lights, but on street corners, darkened parking lots and even at T-junctions in countryside rice fields. And nobody touches them.

There are vending machines for everything. They've got them for sodas, of course, and snacks. There are machines for gum and magazines. Vending machines for cartons of eggs. Vending machines for panty hose and cigarettes. They've even got vending machines for porno magazines and videos on the side of the road.

Vending machines form complete walls on highway rest stops. You can buy instant noodles in Styrofoam cups, octopus balls and even hamburgers, though I don't recommend you do. I was feeling extremely hungry and got a little bit brave and tried it once. They go by the brand name of 'The Guttenburger.' It definitely lived up to its name. I've never eaten a better Gutten in my life, and never plan to again.

But the *coupe de grâce*, is they've got vending machines for ... beer! That's right. Beer. You can buy up to a three-litre can from a vending machine. Now, you tell me how long that would last on some small side street in Anytown, North America.

The interesting thing here is that the drinking age is twenty. So to keep the underaged drinking to a minimum, the beer vending machines are programmed to turn themselves off at eleven p.m. Eleven? More than likely someone set all the timers wrong and the machines were supposed to come on after eleven when most underaged drinkers would be home. Regardless.

The point, getting back to the topic of respect for private and public property, is that these unmonitored machines go untouched by anyone except to fill them up again and replace the Guttens — about once in every five years from what I tasted.

I don't want to paint too rosy a picture however. There are some things in Japan that are scoffed, besides the Momma Charis at the stations. Those being umbrellas. During rainy season, which can result in two months of constant drizzle, citizens are known to knowingly grab umbrellas which are not theirs. Passing by storefronts, they will on occasion, pick one out of the umbrella stands found in front of a store and make their getaway. Ooooo. Umbrella-jacking. Big crime wave there.

I'm not so sure people are necessarily afraid of the authorities and therefore don't tamper with public property. I think that it simply doesn't even enter their minds in the first place.

And that's a good thing.

The 1998 Nagano Winter Olympics (Part One): The Big Show

If you recall, there was a small digital countdown clock over Matsumoto station listing off the number of days until the castle's big birthday do. You may also recall that we hadn't planned on staying to seeing it through. As it turned out, we did. That summer there were all kinds of festivals and fireworks. Laser light shows on the castle grounds at night and a huge expo pavilion was set up near the airport. We had remained in Japan for longer than anticipated, the clock had run out and we were ready to return home.

Then it happened. While we weren't looking, the people of Nagano went out and brought back the Winter Olympics, thereby resetting the clock. Just another 1347 days to go!

No sir. We might have unintentionally stayed to see the first countdown, but this one was too much.

With each passing day, week, year, it got closer and closer. Every time we passed the station it was steadily counting down, almost daring us to stay. Resistance was futile. This was the Olympics. The Big Show, and right in our own backyard. How could we not stay and see zero? So, we promised ourselves once the clock ran out this time, barring any other resettings, we'd return home.

The Winter Olympics held in Nagano in '98 were run

with typical Japanese precision. Olympic President Samaranch announced in his closing speech that the Games were the 'best organized' ever. Not the 'best Games ever' they were hoping for, but considering the fiasco of the Atlanta Games, they'd take it. True, everything was not perfect, but the athletes and media, all agreed that the people of Nagano could not have been more helpful or accommodating. A gold medal for all the volunteers, of which there were many.

It was an excellent ending to what started out as an Olympic event with Olympic-sized problems. The environment was a major stumbling block for the organizers, who promised not to damage any aspects of the natural surroundings. This resulted in many firsts, like the first bobsled course that had an uphill section and the shortest downhill course ever. The downhill headache and ensuing battle between the head of the Nagano Organizing Committee (NOAC), Hayashi san, and the head of the international ski federation (FIS), Marc Hodler, threatened to spoil all the alpine events. If for some reason you didn't hear all this before, the dispute was over the starting gate. In order to make it a truly world-class run, FIS wanted the starting gate to be above 1800 metres. NOAC said 'No.' Mainly because, at that level, the gate would technically be in a national park zone which forbade any professional events to take place in it in order to preserve nature. The kicker for this was that there already were, and still are, two chair lifts running to this height for recreational skiers. It was okay for the average joe to use, but verboten for the pros (or Olympians).

Naturally, neither side would budge. FIS, because they demanded a challenging course and could plainly see that since skiers were already using that area no changes would be needed. And NOAC, simply because if they bent the rules, they would lose face.

There was all kinds of scuttlebutt as to other reasons. Some business people in Hakuba said it was because a rival ski area spent a lot of money trying to get the venue at their mountain. Their changes included chopping down a ton of trees which would have had an adverse affect on the environment, and would have gone into a different national park zone. The environmentalists protested bitterly to NOAC and the proposal was denied. The story goes that the owner of this operation was a little upset, having put a lot of money into this and threatened to stir up the environmental groups and send them to Hakuba if Hakuba was allowed to have the event in the national park zone. Hence NOAC was caught between a rock and a hard place.

Finally, at the eleventh hour, NOAC agreed to a starting point about the same height, but just a few metres outside of the national park zone. This seemed a tad silly as it implied that NAOC was saying that the vegetation a few metres away to the left was less likely to be affected than the vegetation three metres to the right. Anyway, it was a done deal and everyone breathed a little easier. The final peculiar twist to this story is that the intended course crossed over the national park zone shortly after the gate. It would only traverse the zone for approximately four metres, but that was four metres too much. A small jump was made just before the zone so the athletes could sail over that little corner and land outside the national park zone. Anal retentive?

With any event of this magnitude there are bound to be tons of things to work out. Transportation was another canker. Traditional roads were never straight and are inevitably narrow. Now I understand why Japanese cars are so small. Buses would have a hard time to navigate the corners. The distances between the venues were great and usually there was only one road through windy mountain passes, which would make for potentially huge traffic jams. Most stores would not accept foreign credit cards, and bank machines were only open until suppertime. Travellers Cheques? What were those? There weren't going to be enough hotels and those who did get a place to stay might have to contend with a Japanese-style room and toilet, meaning no place to sit in either department. On top of all that, the most fundamental part of any Winter Olympics was painfully absent. The snow. Right up until a month and a half before the Games were to take place, green grass could be seen on large portions of the downhill run. The cross country course was just a track through the forest floor. "That's what you get for having a Winter Olympics this far south," people said. But the *sumo* hadn't sung yet.

Construction carried on at a maddening pace. Roads to venues off the main drags appeared almost overnight. Shuttle buses abounded and the countless volunteers, most of whom started taking government-funded English, German and French lessons two years prior to the Olympics, helped lost souls find their way.

Visa, a main sponsor of the Games, put on a huge push to get shops, restaurants and almost anybody to accept Visa cards from other countries. It wasn't necessarily that the shopkeepers here didn't want to use foreign credit cards per se, but that their card readers were only set up to read Japanese cards. Visa installed new machines and that solved that.

Banks programmed their machines to stay open until 8:30 p.m. I don't know if they didn't realize that they don't have to pay a machine overtime or not, but regardless, they did make some concessions.

Hotels were full but the traditional Japanese inns, called *ryokans,* didn't do as well as hoped. Because most people believed the rumours of room shortages, a lot of Japanese people from other areas didn't bother to check if there were any vacancies. Hence, there were a lot of people who could have gotten rooms that didn't.

As for the snow, what else could they do but pray? And that's exactly what they did.

Members of NOAC went to a Shinto shrine in Hakuba to pray to the weather god. Now, you may find this a little hard to believe in this day and age, in such a modern and high tech country, but it's true. Three days later while the media and people on the street were shaking their heads over such antics, it began to snow. And snow. And snow.

It was unbelievable. Hakuba and the Nagano area got more snow at one time than was ever recorded over the last one hundred years. It wouldn't stop. I guess they prayed too hard.

Though everyone was rejoicing over the snow and the shrine's priest was probably feeling pretty smug, a worry began as to where they were going to put all the snow. Snow plows are in scant supply, as the mountains get snow but the cities don't. A metre and a half of snow in as many days went unplowed in 90% of the streets, making for huge ruts as trucks and cars plowed and pushed their way to work. Construction came to a halt and all vehicles capable of hauling snow were used for just that.

In due course, the streets were cleared and the remaining construction was completed on time.

They built the venues and roads on time and with as little infringement on the environment as promised.

The streets at night were filled with people from around the world. Pedestrians out-numbered cars as they swarmed down side streets waving their country's flags and singing traditional songs at the top of their voices. Every little pub, snack, restaurant and bar was full to overflowing and everyone was smiling. It was truly great. Any time a hockey team won, their national headquarters in town provided free beer and food to celebrate with anyone who cared to join in. That was truly great.

The police, who stated sternly on TV before the Games that they were worried about a higher crime rate with all the foreigners in town, turned into local celebrities. Almost every visitor wanted a picture taken with them in their brightly coloured yellow and blue snow suits and they courteously obliged. During the Games, the same police official was now smiling on TV to announce that even though foreigners used very big actions when speaking, they were extremely polite and that his officers enjoyed having their photos taken.

No one really seemed to mind the line-ups for any kind of transportation and the city remained relatively free of large traffic jams. The blatant advertisements that plagued the ambience of the summer Olympics in Atlanta were purposely missing in Nagano. Because of the extreme distance, there were relatively few foreign street vendors, and there basically are no Japanese street vendors, so those who ventured all the way over to Japan made a fortune. Pin sellers earned up to $3000 a day from eager Japanese Olympics crazed citizens. Their business was so lucrative that many stayed through the summer.

It was a two week festival of international sport, but also international friendship. The normally xenophobic people of Nagano couldn't get enough of the foreign visitors. They had invited the world to come, and the world came.

The 1998 Nagano Winter Olympics (Part Two): A Brush with 'Great'ness

Because of my full-time job I could not get as much time off as I would have liked to see the events. I also didn't have that much money. Olympic tickets generally sell at Olympian prices. We did get tickets to see an ice hockey game, and traded in some other tickets plus a little cash to a British scalper, to see the men's short program in figure skating. My family is enthralled with Canada's Elvis Stoijko. Not only because of his obvious talent, but because they think I look remarkably like him. John McEnroe or Elvis Stoijko. Never Mel Gibson or Brad Pitt.

Anyway, before the Games English speaking-reporters were in short supply. Being a freelancer for radio and print publications, I was a relatively hot commodity. National CBC Radio, *USA TODAY* online and *Maclean's* magazine were looking for a local perspective and I was it. During the Games I was kept busy with my own Olympic website, *USA TODAY* online, and continued to keep my home turf of Atlantic Canada up to date on the behind-the-scenes happenings via reports for CBC Radio.

As a buildup to the Games, I mentioned that I was particularly excited to see Canada play hockey, as I had always wanted to see Wayne Gretzky play. I said during one pre-

Olympic interview how I remembered delivering newspapers one winter evening in my hometown of Moncton, New Brunswick. It was freezing cold and to occupy myself, I read the paper under each passed street light. As I walked into the glow of the next lamp, I saw a picture of this young kid, about three years older than I was, smiling away. The caption read, "Wayne Gretsky Signs Whatever Million Deal over a Whatever Year Period." 'Whatever million!' I thought to myself. I'd be smiling too, for that. As I trudged home past the lake, I just couldn't believe that someone could get that much money for playing hockey. He must be good. And at almost the same age as me. Next to his salary, my Christmas tips didn't seem like such a big deal anymore.

So now, some seventeen years later, I'd get a chance to see him play on the other side of the world. Both of us a long way from home, and him probably still making more money than me.

The plan was that I would call the radio station during the game on my cellular phone to say how things were going and to give my impression of seeing The Great One play live. It was good for me, and it was bad for me.

After having lived here for eight years I knew the time difference between Japan and the East Coast pretty well. Yet, it was I who screwed up on when the station was going to call. Because cellular phones were not allowed in the main stadium, I had to leave Caroline alone while I waited to be rung. Most of the game I spent peering over people's shoulders trying to catch a glimpse of Gretzky. Finally the phone rang, forty-five minutes later than expected. I answered it in the hallway.

It was the sound engineer. He wanted to get a sound level before going live with the host. That done, he said the producer would call me back in ten and hung up. I was getting a little agitated, to say the least, that they were keeping me waiting while the game was going on. I brought all my expensive camera equipment so I could get a good shot of Wayne, but had to leave it all up to Caroline as she watched without me.

While I stood silently fuming away, the echoing sound of boot heels clicking down the corridor could be heard. I looked up. Walking right past me was American figure-skating star Kristie Yamaguchi on her way to the washroom. Wow. Going to the bathroom just like the rest of us would. I reached down for my camera, which I had been lugging around all day to ask for a photo, but it wasn't there. It never fails to happen. Whenever you want to have your picture taken with a famous person, your wife has your camera. Still, seeing someone so famous walk by when only you are there was pretty neat, I thought. Worth the wait I suppose.

So now the producer called back and I forgot about Kristie and got back to being a little steamed.

"Why didn't you call me on time?"

"I am."

"What?"

"You said you were thirteen hours ahead, right?"

"Oh yeah. Ha ha. Sorry."

The interview went on without a hitch and when we wrapped it up, I was told that a different station wanted to talk to me after the game and could I wait. No problem. Glad to oblige.

The game was over and Canada won handily 5 to 1. It was a good game but I was a little disappointed in not having seen more of it. I paid the exorbitant price of the tickets to see Gretzky play, but spent much of the time waiting in the corridor. Seeing Kristie on her way to the washroom was a bonus, but not what I came for.

The stadium emptied. Caroline and I met up with some friends outside to take the shuttle bus back to the train station together. I told them I had to take one more call from another CBC station and would meet them at the shuttle stop. Not wanting to monkey around with my camera equipment during the interview, I asked Caroline if she would take my stuff with her. Ever helpful, she did.

By this time, the stadium was empty and most everyone had gone on their way. I was standing on a second level entrance way where I seemed to get the best reception for my phone. The radio station called, said they had a good line, and put me on hold. While I was waiting, I could hear the show in progress. I could hear the host talking of school bus delays because of heavy snow in areas I knew as a kid. I was standing outside the stadium, listening live to a local radio show from home, on the earpiece of a phone the size of a small remote control, on the other side of the world. Amazing.

My turn came and went. I talked about seeing a little of Wayne, a lot of Kristie and the general happenings of a small city hosting the Olympics. In about five minutes, it was all over and I hit the 'off' button. Smiling, and feeling a little homesick, I turned around to catch up with Caroline at the bus stop. I froze in my tracks. Yea, but ten feet away, and just through an open door at the base of a stairwell, who should be there but the Great One himself and his lovely wife Janet.

Gack! I couldn't believe. For the second time that night I reached down for a camera that just wasn't there. *Bwaaaaah!* I want my camera! I moved inside the building, about three feet away, to join the small group that had gathered around. Without a doubt, I looked like an idiot. My face was starting to go numb from my stupid grin and my teeth were getting dry. My brain flashed a mental image of what I must look like, but I ignored it and kept on. I was standing next to the Great One and his Missus. Mr. and Mrs. Great One. I didn't say a word. They probably said afterwards some time later, "Did you see that guy just standing there grinning? Poor sap. Probably there with some kind of group program."

Both Janet and Wayne were talking to the now infamous snowboarder Ross Rebigliati, who earlier that day lost his gold medal. At first I thought maybe a deal was going down, but then I realized I was talking about Wayne here and knew this not to be true. After some signatures and some encouraging words to the snowboarder, Wayne and Janet disappeared into a room on the other side of the corridor. I stepped back out into the cold as the rest of the hangers-on talked to Ross.

Wow. Quite an eventful night. Two interviews, two stars and a hockey game to boot. I could only think of one thing: "Why in the hell did I keep giving my camera away!"

The Olympics finished on a cold gray day with spectacular fireworks at night. Everyone deemed it a great success, which it was. It was great to be here to see it all from the beginning, and to see Nagano transformed into a place that is now a little more understanding of the world and the people in it.

For us, the ending of the Olympics felt like the ending of a great book. One reason we didn't want it to be over was because it would mean that we ourselves would be leaving soon. But now, the clock over the station has been turned off for almost a year. A silent reminder of the promise we made to ourselves to go home when it was. For a variety of reasons that are personal to us, we both know it's time and are making plans for our return.

Originally, on that very first day of our arrival at Narita airport, we reiterated to ourselves that if we could come to Japan, stay a year, return home and break even, we'd be ahead of the game. By the time we come home for good in the spring of '99, that one year will have stretched into nine. And what will that make us? Rich! That's what. I'm only kidding. Not monetarily anyway, but definitely rich in terms of experiences.

It will be hard to leave the friends, the places we know, the fun of living abroad and the mountains. But we look forward to what lies ahead and all the new experiences it will bring. Especially when we originally arrived at Narita with two, but arc leaving with three. That'll be another story, for another time.

For now, let me say in advance, it's good to be home, and hopefully, we'll see you soon.

Thank You's

Where to begin? Hmm. More than likely only the people who know me personally or have had any contact with Caroline or me over the last nine years, will read the 'Thanks You's' just to see if they're mentioned or not. I'll have to be diplomatic. Thank you everyone! There.

This started a few years ago with friends Warren and James saying I should write down the stories I told them on the phone. One night, when I locked myself out of the house, I sat at a counter in a coffee shop and started doing just that with paper and pencil. After much finagling it was done in its first form and read for review and critiqued by my sister Heather MacAuley, and friends Michael Dunn, James Small and Betty Szo. After revisions galore and tweaking, the final draft went to Mike Granville, English teacher and high school drama director extraordinaire. Many thanks to him.

Also thanks to the good folks at Community Books, especially to Brenda Conroy for her diligence in making everything just right with the book even on the weekends and Kathleen Tudor for answering endless questions to a stranger via email.

The most thanks go to my wife Caroline who went through all of it with me. She read and reread every revision, steering me in the right direction the whole time, and still even managed to laugh in the right places.

About the Cover Photos

The front cover photo is taken from the pyramid-like peak of Yarigatake, the second highest peak in the Japanese Northern Alps. Climbing partner, Takuya Yokoyama, and I made the 3180-metre ascent in one day to the top and back. Perhaps, the only ones EVER to do that (ahem ahem). We used the elevator. Just kidding. Actually, we cheated a bit by using our mountain bikes along the flatter bottom section from the entrance of Kamikochi Park. After that, we locked our bikes to some trees and up we went. The last leg of our return was in the dark, and riding out on our hobbled knees was not a pleasure. A once and lifetime thing. Reminiscent of climbing Mt. Fuji. The view (and wind) were phenomenal, but I don't think I'd want to do it again.

The back cover photo is from Mount Jonen — the fifth highest peak (2983 metres)and across the valley from Yarigatake. A much nicer experience and you could drive your car more than half way. Now that's the way to climb.